Edward Payson

The Law of Equivalents in it's Relation to Political and Social Ethics

Edward Payson

The Law of Equivalents in it's Relation to Political and Social Ethics

ISBN/EAN: 9783744666947

Printed in Europe, USA, Canada, Australia, Japan

Cover: Foto ©Suzi / pixelio.de

More available books at **www.hansebooks.com**

THE

LAW OF EQUIVALENTS

IN ITS RELATION TO POLITICAL AND
SOCIAL ETHICS

BY

EDWARD PAYSON

"*Frustra fit per plura,
Quod fieri fas erat per pauciora*"

BOSTON AND NEW YORK
HOUGHTON, MIFFLIN AND COMPANY
The Riverside Press, Cambridge
1888

Copyright, 1888,
By EDWARD PAYSON.

All rights reserved.

The Riverside Press, Cambridge:
Electrotyped and Printed by H. O. Houghton & Co.

PREFACE.

THE following treatise is semi-philosophical, semi-practical. In the sense first named, it is offered to the public, not professing to present any new discoveries, but under the belief that certain long known and familiar truths, which till now have been recognized only under a disconnected and isolated form, by being collocated and brought into juxtaposition, may exert an influence more in proportion to their intrinsic claims than they have hitherto done. In other departments the value of classification is well understood and readily acknowledged. An orderly grouping and systematic arrangement of scattered, unassorted facts is always esteemed a valuable auxiliary towards the establishment of principles; and every process of well-founded generalization furnishes a new stepping-stone in the pursuit of truth, greatly aiding and expediting the researches of subsequent explorers.

A somewhat similar acquisition is reached when, without attempting to evolve a new principle, we refer certain experiences and certain results, which have hitherto had, so to speak, only a nomadic existence, to a single, uniform law. So far as we succeed in doing this, we may, if nothing more, narrow somewhat the domain of accident, encourage more exact habits of thought, and by this massing of separate truths, exchange the inefficiency of a rabble, delivering its blows and directing its steps at random, for a marshalled, orderly army under a recognized leader. It remains to consider wherein the treatise is practical.

It can hardly have failed to attract the notice of sincere and thoughtful minds, how civilization, especially on these American shores, is to-day demanding great things in the moral world; great changes in social life, even to magnificence; while it is certainly not less noteworthy, how it is at the same time expecting to receive them from great sources, themselves equally magnificent. Men are not only hoping to find God,— that is, to get away from the pains and the penalties and the weaknesses incident to humanity, — but now, too, more than ever, they think to find Him "in the whirlwind," and not " in the still, small voice." Calculating and shrewd and sagacious as the American mind confessedly is in all matters of trade and commerce, in all departments that are physical as opposed to spiritual, it is full unto fullness, even as the sea is full, with romantic hopes, and romantic endeavor, and romantic machinery, whenever it turns its attention to what is spiritual, or moral, or social, and not physical or material. The great inconsequence of this day and generation is its solid sense here, its wild romance there; its cautious, inquisitive, questioning spirit, where its secular interests are involved, and where certain points of mere speculative belief are concerned; and its easy credulity where great changes and sweeping reforms are contemplated in social life. In the same breath it pays its homage to law, and degrades law to a level with the caprice of accident. It walls itself about and insures itself against loss with a forecasting sagacity and a careful balancing of competitive claims whenever its worldly substance is in jeopardy; for protection against injury where great social interests are at stake, it throws itself blindly and confidingly into the arms of whatever guide chances first to turn up on the crowded thoroughfare. On Wall Street, on 'Change everywhere, dazzle counts but little; elsewhere, nothing attains very high repute without dazzle. Only let some newly arrived nostrum be loudly heralded and promise enough, and then let it be organized with all pomp of circumstance, and get itself placarded with a few favorite names, and its success is a foregone conclusion. How much will it accomplish? is a question quite sure to be asked; how certain the results, is seldom inquired into.

And since great things are expected, it is only the natural concomitant of this state of mind that great and pretentious instrumentalities are counted upon to bring them about. Acts of Congress, decisions of learned judges; legislation, with all its technical forms and imposing ceremony; cumbrous apparatus of associated enterprise, holding its annual meetings under blare of trumpets, flare of banners with emblematic device, and what not other pageantry, — these, and like unto these, captivate the minds of vast numbers who seek relief for a past disappointment in the hope that the next venture will bring a prize, and who thus continually flatter themselves that the bright spot is only a stone's throw in advance, which, with one good strong pull together at the oars, we shall presently shoot ahead sheer into.

This inconsequence in the American mind — this romance dwelling side by side with a practical, common-sense element — may be, in part at least, referred to certain patent causes of which it is the natural, logical sequence : it is the product of contagion. It happens by the transfer of certain principles and habits of thought from a field where they are legitimate over into a different field, where they have no proper application, are indefensible, and are attended with most mischievous consequences. The American mind, in a degree far beyond what ever happened before, has been made to contemplate, and has become familiarized with magnitude everywhere, and with rapid growth and astonishing results everywhere. No other elements have entered so largely into American civilization as these. A continent washed by two oceans furnished the field for its evolutions. Its rivers coursed thousands of miles before reaching their outlet. Its mountains raised their heads to the clouds, while the treasures that since the birth of Time had been slumbering in their bosoms were now unlocked as if by the hand of a mighty enchanter. And vast as was the field, vaster still was the enterprising spirit which had now come to preside over and subdue it. If it did not span the ocean with a bridge, nor take it up in its hands as a very little thing, it stood upon the margin and united two hemispheres in instantaneous thought; to that extent fulfilling its boast that it would annihilate space. So everywhere all about it. Cities sprung up at its feet. Palaces rose up in a night. The fable of the wonderful "Lamp of Aladdin" was realized. Genii more powerful than they of the Lamp have been evoked; the wonders of fable have been surpassed.

Witnessing all this, themselves the actors, too, and participating in the fruits, is it strange that men should expect to find a similar law of growth in moral science, and should count upon results equally grand, equally rapid? Is it to be wondered at that romantic hopes are indulged, that romantic schemes are devised, that the unthinking are cajoled by false promises, that in the minds of many scepticism is begotten of frequent failure, that the little we might secure is hopelessly lost by demanding too much, that where progress is most of all needed, there the world stands still, if it does not retrograde?

With this explanation of the design the author has proposed to himself, he hopes that a want of unity, or any defect that may be detected which would justly expose him to rebuke at the hands of a technical, rigid criticism, will be regarded more leniently by the public at large, to whose judgment the following pages are submitted.

TABLE OF CONTENTS.

CHAPTER		PAGE
I.	STATEMENT OF THE LAW	1
II.	INEXORABLENESS OF THE LAW IN ITS DEMAND FOR PERSONAL PAYMENT	35
III.	COMMENDABLE CHARACTER OF AN ENTERPRISE NOT A GUARANTY OF ITS SUCCESS	50
IV.	ROMANCE AS INFECTING THEOLOGY	62
V.	LEGISLATION ONLY SUPPLEMENTAL AS AN AID TO REFORMS	76
VI.	POLITICAL OR GOVERNMENTAL EQUIVALENTS	85
VII.	ANTITHETICAL EQUIVALENTS	113
VIII.	FINELY MODULATED SCALE OF EQUIVALENTS	139
IX.	UNCONSCIOUS PAYMENTS	150
X.	NO EQUIVALENT FOR CONTENTMENT	154
XI.	IN CERTAIN DEPARTMENTS CLASSIFIED AS ORGANIC, SPECIAL LIMITATIONS HAVE BEEN IMPOSED	167
XII.	VARIEGATED SOURCES OF CIVILIZATION	178
XIII.	SOME UNIVERSAL EQUIVALENTS — TIME	182
XIV.	THOUGHT	189
XV.	PURITY	197
XVI.	PERSONALITY	207
XVII.	WOMAN SUFFRAGE	221
XVIII.	THE FAMILY INSTITUTION — WHEREIN THE FAMILY DIFFERS FROM SOCIETY	255
XIX.	WHEREIN THE FAMILY DIFFERS FROM THE STATE	267
XX.	WHEREIN THE FAMILY DIFFERS FROM THE SCHOOL	270
XXI.	WHEREIN THE FAMILY DIFFERS FROM THE CHURCH	276
XXII.	CONCLUSION OF FAMILY INSTITUTION	283
XXIII.	EDUCATION — ARSENALS OF LEARNING	288
XXIV.	RESULTS	302

THE LAW OF EQUIVALENTS.

CHAPTER I.

STATEMENT OF THE LAW.

SUCCESS — Failure. For man, what more significant, what more comprehensive words than these? Words, too, which, as to a possible class of sentient creatures superior to man, we may suppose to be, and which, as to the external world, organic and inorganic, that surrounds man, we know to be, quite insignificant; that is, without meaning or interest of any sort. Of all the multiform and manifold antitheses which offer themselves for our study and amusement, is not this the chief? nay, to declare the whole question, is not this the sum? Having included within this field all that belongs to it, what remains? Vast area of debatable ground enclosed between these antipodal extremes, lies there any territory beyond them, already subdued and put under cultivation by man; any possible *terra incognita* even, which he thinks of subduing at some future time? Quite evidently not. As of all past endeavor, whether of yesterday, and so standing out clearly revealed to our eyes in bold, sharp-angled relief; or of a remoter age, and so its outline somewhat dim and shadowy, the sole question is, did it succeed — did it fail; in like manner of all possible future undertakings, the single inquiry is, shall it succeed — shall it fail?

And it is both curious and painful to observe how, undeterred by our lamentable failure to find logical and hence unanimous explanation of these opposite results, even when the undertaking is of the past, its inner mechanism, and its workings and strugglings towards completion thus laid open to our inspection, and the task, as would seem, thereby made easy for us, we in no wise abate our efforts, or restrain our hopes, that hereafter we shall be more wise and more fortunate; and accordingly with the certainty that belongs to law, predict success or failure of this inchoate enterprise, whose workings and whose inner mechanism are still all unrevealed. In other words, we amuse ourselves with the hope that we shall in good time arrive at the point of predicting certain results of the future, when it is but too evident that to-day we cannot even explain, or at least do not agree in explaining, a similar class of results which are of the past. In matters where, thus far, we have displayed our incompetency as teachers, we now seek to be prophets — to be revealers where hitherto we have failed to be illustrators.

And that men do not abate their efforts or chasten their hopes in this regard — that in imagination, at least, they behold placed in their hands the one sole, legitimate key for this Bramah lock of many wards to be presently substituted with happiest results for the surreptitious keys which have long hung suspended from the girdle of pretentious locksmiths and lock-pickers — is evident enough. For why otherwise give audience at all to the innumerable tribe of vaticinators, or rather soothsayers — for, be it observed, this latter word includes as possible in its signification, not only a sayer of truth, but a sayer of pleasing things also, as, indeed, it ought, when we consider by whom it has been appropriated — why give audience to these who so loudly and so confidently predict a "better time coming"? If there be better things in store for us, if the better time coming, so long heralded as close at hand, prove not in the coming years the same illusive *ignis fatuus* it has proved in the years that are past, such change must happen to us by reason of redeeming somewhat, somewhere, from the domain of accident and conjecture, and referring the same to some fixed but hitherto unobserved or at least unapplied law.

If not upon such new discovery, or upon the more full recognition of some such law, where, we may ask, does rest the foundation of these hopeful predictions? If to "Count Cagliostros" and "Madame Le Normands" — if to magicians, and necromancers, and astrologers, and clairvoyants, with all their paraphernalia of divining-rods, and crucibles, and sulphurous fumes, and what not other devices — if to these and such as these we are to look for guidance — if we are still shut up to such altogether inarticulate, ambiguous oracles to learn whether success or failure waits upon the newly launched enterprise, how may we at all hope for other results than those which have happened to us aforetime? No. When we make that certain which has hitherto been uncertain, we secure a new instrument of progress, and, not irrationally, may count upon making, with greater or less, with more rapid or slower strides, an advance. So far as what has hitherto rested in conjecture, even if it be the conjecture of the wisest man, or of all wisest men united, comes instead thereof to rest in demonstration, so far a step is gained. Then, we need have no fear lest the light that is in us be darkness. Then, we need not be disturbed, fearing that we have kindled our beacon on some floating Delos island, which, instead of guiding the truthful navigator into port, shall betray him to destruction.

Now the question which salutes us at the very threshold is this: Is there any general, fixed law whatever appertaining to this matter of success — failure, which, in virtue of its being more formally and distinctly announced, and so more fully recognized and acted upon than has been hitherto done, promises to contribute, in a slight degree even, towards making that certain which to-day, of all things whatever, seems most uncertain? There is a law of gravitation, a law of combustion, each making certain what would otherwise be all uncertain, knowing which, men escape much they would, if ignorant of this law, be exposed to. Is there in any similar sense a law of success, to be termed, shall we say, the "Law of Equivalents," which, once reduced into formal possession, we may better give heed to, and so be less exposed to disappointment and other untoward consequences, which, as of one sort and another they result from the neglect of all laws, so must attend upon the infraction of this law? Does this foundling, hitherto, as would seem, not deemed worthy of a name at all, deserve the name we have given him? Admit that we may raise him up out of the ditch into which he has fallen, and bestow upon him such decent apparel as shall prove to be at hand, to thus make him, after a fashion, presentable. Is it quite certain we are not arrogating for him a name beyond his deserts? Is he of such lofty lineage, such honorable extraction, that he can be said to belong at all to the family into which we now propose to introduce him?

Pertinent questions these, for consider a moment how much is included under this word "law." What is law but uniformity? and for man, whose many weaknesses and tender infirmities and proneness to stumble would seem to require soft and cottony swaddling-clothes, whose pliant folds should have thought for, and accommodate themselves to, this infantile unsteadiness of his — we say, for man, what more terrible word than this — this hard, angular, inexorable uniformity? There is no dandling, no caressing, no soothing lullaby here; but, instead thereof, rude, rough handling, as of some hirsute, untonsured giant, with grasp like a vice — a letting fall, nay, rather a dashing-down to the frozen earth of this limp babyhood, with nonchalance almost devilish — this, or something like this, is what we are made to look upon, when we consider and ask ourselves what is the full significance of this word "law" — uniformity; and we ask again, what more terrible word for man than this? And since all law, however it may differ in that it has to do now with matters of less, now of higher value, always agrees in this — that it is uniform, inexorable, and so in this sense all law is of equal dignity and significance, it beseems us well to take good heed lest we carelessly appropriate the word even, and so, calling that law which is only accident, invest a mere pretender with the royal purple that belongs to the king only.

Is there, then, anything in this matter of equivalents which can justly claim to be called a law? As remarked already, there is a law of gravitation in no wise to be relaxed or suspended in behalf of the unwary traveller who sets his foot too near the crumbling edge of the precipice. There is a law of combustion, and though whole cities may suffer from it, and the wealth men have been gathering up through long years of toil and self-denial melt away from them in a single night, by reason of a spark falling a hand's breadth to the right rather than to the left, there is no help for it — the law must be satisfied. It may be a great army has been marshalled and equipped, under some lately-Corsican adventurer — now become French emperor — and the earth trembles beneath their feet, as the moving squadrons take their way towards yon Russian capital. Soon follows Borodino battle — Russian capital is given to the flames. Beyond that circle of fire lies, in half-concealed ambush, another foe — the piercing cold of a northern winter — and the ominous word " retreat " is sounded all along through those now broken ranks. Retreat! Back again, through deserts where there are no houses, and no food grows; where is wide, interminable sweep of half-frozen marsh and stainless snow; stainless now, but tomorrow to be crimsoned with the blood of that fugitive host whose course is marked by the bodies of dead and dying soldiers. Back again? Yes, even to the banks of some opposing Beresina river, whose thronged bridge, hammered upon by close-pursuing Russian artillery, shall then and there fall in pieces, and in the coming spring twelve thousand corpses shall tell how many French fighting-men, in one single instant, found watery graves there. Back again? Yes; and out of all that mighty host, preyed upon by disease, and famine, and cold, and fatigue, and the bayonets of the pursuing foe, twenty thousand are at last gathered under the walls of Paris. Such is law!

See that widowed mother there. Except for that single son of hers, that only child, her daily prayer would be to go hence, and join the father of that child, now, as she believes, in heaven. But the son remains, a support and a solace to the mother — the mother a support and solace to the son. When the labors of the day are over, the mother already watching there with listening ear for the familiar footfall, he hurries away from the place of business, the path he follows showing, just a step in advance, a decrepit, shivering, starving, friendless beggar. The report of a rifle, carelessly handled and discharged, is heard; the beggar passes on unharmed; the listening ear hears not one impatient footstep, but many, as of a crowd, that hesitates; and she knows it all. Law — law even in accident.

But assuming, as we for a moment must, that there is no misappropriation of the word here — be it so. What of it? Why not allow the foundling thus lying, naked and nameless, under the hedge to remain there? Why call for christening robes, and, by giving the outcast a name, make his worthlessness perhaps all the more apparent? To which questions we now proceed to furnish such answer as may be; premising only this one quite self-evident remark — that lofty endeavor is often attended by miserable failure; that lavish expenditure is daily and hourly followed by most pitiful results; the fit solution of which apparent incongruousness, we flatter ourselves we have found, when, taking up with that which comes accredited to us by long usage, we exclaim: Fortune is a blind goddess, a capricious, perverse dame, who bestows her favors altogether at random. And we pronounce this man lucky, and that man unlucky; and that is all there is to be said about it.

Let us, then, now inquire, the way having thus been prepared for it, what is meant by this "law of equivalents." A man chances upon a horse having certain fine points, offered for sale in the market, and would like to become the owner of him. He feels well assured that one or two, or five hundred, or, it may be, that five thousand dollars will not answer the purpose; but he is equally well assured that, somewhere along in the line of hundreds or thousands, there is a point he can reach, so that his purse be long enough, when the coveted object may become his own. Another man goes into the market to buy a barrel of flour. He understands perfectly well that the only question which can arise is, whether, supposing, indeed, that his money be not counterfeit, he has enough of it. It is a question of quantity, and nothing else. And so always, all along through the narrow, intricate by-ways where trade and commerce engage men's attention — in all the infinitely diversified pursuits and transactions where the sole object of the transfer is money, from the wholesale millionaire, who buys by the cargo, down to the poor needle-woman, who sends to the retail shop on the corner for a half ounce of tea, it is still and always a question of amount, and nothing else. And inasmuch as ninety-nine parts in a hundred of all that occupies the thoughts and furnishes motive to the vast majority, is this very kind of exchange we have described, money to be paid by one party and received by the other, the quantity thereof being the sole question; and inasmuch as almost every man in the community is reminded of this fact by every money transaction he enters into, and so has it dwelling by his side every day and every hour of his life, would it not be the most natural error in the world for him to fall into, that the same rule applies elsewhere, quite outside of money transactions? Might we not suspect, even were there no recorded facts to demonstrate it, that in other calculations, and other enterprises, quite foreign to those of trade and commerce, he would be found still placing his reliance on, and making sole account of, quantity, amount, magnitude, in matters with which, if the truth were to be spoken, all these have nothing and less than nothing to do?

We have thus selected money and given to it a

prominence here, since, having been long accepted by common consent as the measure of value, it seemed the fittest illustration for the purpose in hand. But it is as an illustration only that we have introduced it, and not at all as an exhaustive statement of the subject-matter. For the commodities or objects to which the measure is to be applied — how are these in turn to be themselves estimated? Chiefly again by bulk, by magnitude, by quantity — all these, or some of them, to be ascertained and set down with counting-house exactness on the appointed page, so many pounds troy or avoirdupois — so many cubic feet, so many bushels. And this is not accident, and so forming an exception to a rule. It is not accident, and so a matter against which relief is to be sought or prayed for. Within its legitimate sphere it is itself legitimate. It is the law of man's condition, who, himself the subject of material wants, has been constituted lord and proprietor of a material universe. In the fashioning and subduing of this universe, he not only makes provision for these his natural wants, which haunt him at every step, clamoring loudly to be satisfied, but here he wins almost his only triumphs. Here he is allowed to witness a growth commensurate with the amount of skill and labor expended, and in this growth and these triumphs he imagines, at least, that he discovers approbation for the path his industry has selected — chiefly, material; secondarily, spiritual.

Again, outside and beyond the mammon temple, around whose walls forever ascends the roar of trade and commerce, a still additional contribution, though of a quite opposite description, is found in the same direction in our emotions. Illimitable stretch of far-sweeping forests; stupendous cataracts; immense lakes; snow-capped mountains; immeasurable, ever-booming ocean; those mysterious orbs of light that pursue their way through the unfathomable vault above us — all these awaken within us emotions of sublimity. They fill us with delight; they claim our homage; they penetrate our souls with a religious awe. However the mere arithmetic of life, which has to do with the inferior parts of man's nature, may have hanging around it a taint of the sordid, and the gross, and the sensual, no conscience-questions arise in this school to annoy the willing disciple. In yielding to these emotions, instead of any fear lest he may be approaching dangerous ground, he feels that he is responding to a voice that addresses his better nature, inviting him to a purer atmosphere, to loftier heights, to brighter fields. And thus, once more, magnitude becomes for us at the same time a synonym and a symbol of value. The great is the good; the vast is the sacred; the infinite is the holy. And surely it were passing strange if habits of thought become so inveterate by long indulgence, and by constant exercise; if rules of measurement, so incorporated and interfused into our very life by a strict necessity of our nature, by the very law of its being, and then still further accredited by these higher and holier instincts, — passing strange would it be if principles thus introduced to our hands should never overleap their appropriate boundaries, and be found claiming an application in other fields to which they are all unsuited.

Reduced, then, to set formula, the law means, first, this: that for a large class of objects which the world has long set its heart upon, — indeed, for most that are not subjects of trade, — nature affixes as the price, not magnitude, not amount, not quantity, not even value, as men estimate value, but kind — specific reward being attached to specific effort, and specific experience to specific payment.

Secondly. As payment must be made in kind, the law is inexorable, and recognizes nothing like barter or substitution — knows nothing of exchangeable values.

Thirdly. Insisting as it does upon kind, the law takes into its own hands the decision as to what that kind shall be, and determines beyond appeal its value; and, although it frequently demands variety of payment, it accepts no surplus endowments or offerings in one direction, to atone for lack in another.

We thus state the proposition in set phrase, and with what may possibly be deemed stately and ostentatious parade. We bestow upon it the dignity, the importance, and the full significance of a fundamental, primal law, arrogating for it all that this word "law" ever includes; its neglect or violation to bring upon us no less loss, no less positive detriment, than does the neglect or violation of any law whatever. We believe it will be found to deserve the rank we thus claim for it. But it is, at the same time, capable of being stated in a more simple, or at least less pretentious, form when its meaning becomes this: that humble, and what to our careless apprehension seem altogether contemptible and insignificant, agencies are often the real, the true, the pregnant sources of our advancement; that nature, irrespective of any dogmatic estimates of ours, and quite heedless of our preconceived notions, awards a value, and attaches a consequence, to these so-called "little things," which she will have acknowledged, and which we must ourselves, in the end, recognize and convert to our service, before we can attain to the full stature of which we are capable; that whether success shall attend our efforts, often turns upon exceedingly minute and apparently worthless points, but points, for all that, none the less rigorously insisted upon. A man may spend his whole life in the effort, but he shall never reduce the lump of gold to a perfect sphere by the strokes of a hammer. He may imagine he has done so, after great expenditure of labor to that end, but the microscope shall detect his error, and so, in the world of matter, an instance be afforded to illustrate the "law of equivalents." In a word, its intention is to direct man's attention away from what is pretentious, and frequently nothing more than that; from what is vast, and frequently as vague as it is vast, and admired of us because it is vague; from what gives uncertain promise of magnificent results, to that which gives sure and covenanted reward — covenanted to us by all the undeviating uniformity and inviolable sacredness of law itself.

As illustrative of the foregoing remarks, perhaps nothing would better reward our search than certain facts lying upon the surface which meet us at every turn. A law of life or of healthy growth has been violated. The statesman has overwrought that active brain of his; the sensualist has fallen into helplessness, perhaps idiocy, by his free indulgences; the laborer, perhaps head of a family, to contribute more generously to the comfort of those who are dependent upon him, has taxed his physical energies beyond the point of healthfulness. To be restored, what is the one, sole equivalent each of these must bring in his hands? Repentance, not in any theologic sense, but a return — a retracing of their steps along the same path by which they were severally led to the catastrophe: for the laborer and the statesman, rest; for the sensualist, abstinence. So of a state or people who have lapsed into imbecility;

but one Ariadnean thread conducts out from the labyrinth. In all these cases we understand perfectly well that the price of restoration is a question of kind, and not of amount. And still more heartily do we testify to the same truth when we rebuke the inconsiderate, unseasonable zeal which would repay days and weeks of starvation with instant abundance.

The analogical, and so, if not demonstrative, at least corroborative, illustration which physical science furnishes in the material world, is still more abundant. And of this description, perhaps, there is none more curious than that which is afforded by the laws of light. An experiment said to have been performed by Sir William Herschell is in point. On preparing a solar spectrum, and so decomposing and dividing the different colored rays each from the other, and then exposing a thermometer to each of them in turn, he confidently expected to find the most marked result in the yellow space, which was the brightest; and great was his surprise on finding, not only that this was not true, but that the greatest effect of all was produced at the furthest remove from the yellow, and, indeed, quite beyond the red — which occupied the extreme space — even to where the light ceased to be visible at all. And in another similar experiment, where not heat, but chemical action, was looked for, a similar disappointment was the result. So, too, a like surprise has probably happened to some of us, on learning for the first time that glass, which so freely transmits heat from the sun's rays, intercepts the artificial heat which comes from our own firesides. But, in the case just mentioned of the spectrum, instead of the greatest heat being found at its centre, where the light was the strongest, it was there precisely that the effect was smallest, both as to heat and chemical forces — a fact which possibly certain modern experimenters in the field of moral science would do well to make a note of.

As another hardly less curious illustration might be cited the well-known fact, that there is inherent in soils found only here and there a quality which imparts a certain flavor — often highly prized — to plants and vines grown therein, which is looked for in vain elsewhere. Nor is the rule confined to plants which gratify the palate, but it has a wider range, and the cotton manufacturer knows very well where to apply when he requires for his purpose a fibre of exceptional strength and fineness. But no chemist, however skilled, can detect the occult element lurking there which brings about the magic result; nor can he produce from his laboratory anything the addition of which to the less favored soil shall bestow upon it the peculiar qualities which belong to that identical one — its proud and preappointed rival.

> ... "But in another country, as he said,
> Bore a bright golden flower, but not in this soil."
> MASK OF COMUS.

And it might be here remarked, that agricultural chemistry and heart chemistry are not very wide apart as to the limitations they are severally subject to. Much, as would seem, remains to be done in both of these departments, before Nature's minute subdivisions and careful adjustments are thoroughly understood, or the fine lines she pursues are fully comprehended.

See this cloyed, limp voluptuary. How vain are his longings to taste once more the pleasures which a few years ago made life so pleasant to him! In what a painful, perplexed state of hovering does he not find himself, unable to fix a choice anywhere; in some half-lucid interval almost wishing himself that hod-carrier yonder, so that he only had his full complement of life — his rounded muscle and fierce appetite!

This other child, nursed in the lap of ease, quite unsuspecting as to the great wrong that has been practised upon him — could he, by some miraculous interposition in his behalf, be made to understand by how much he is the sufferer in that he can never know the sweets of triumph over difficulties — what might not he afford to give, so that he were allowed to put forth his hand and pluck some of this pleasant fruit? But the child that cries for the moon shall have his desire as soon as this one.

For it is to be observed, that in all these cases where this price in kind, and not quantity, is exacted, payment must be made by the party who is to be benefited, and not by his friends for him — a strict condition which seems all the greater hardship because it is very often the man's friends only who see clearly wherein he lacks and wherein he is overladen; while he himself is mole-blind as to the weakness — that is to say, his blindness is not only complete, but natural or congenital. "We wanted to get at him and give him a good shaking," — have we not, most of us, heard such remark in relation to some third party, who, balancing on the very edge of success, seemed to need but the slightest possible jostle or hint to tip him quite over into the very lap of fruition? " If this friend of ours only had the least bit more heartiness, or even outside animation;" "Were this one just a trifle more pliable;" "If this other will insist upon being so singularly honest, could he not be so in a less blunt and offensive way, with a little more gracefulness?" — these remarks, and others like them, we are made to listen to constantly; those who make them not considering that the arrangement is an entire one, and that all tinkering is excluded, at least by strangers. " What a pity it seems that these two may not be fused and mixed together!" — a simple enough way to make surplus here pay for deficiency there, and full of promise, too; if so be, by any chemical process lately arrived at and patented, this mingling, and so averaging, of two, as at present constituted, unprofitable characters, could be thus safely and expeditiously compassed. This life chemistry, were it but once reduced into our possession, as is that other which busies itself with the inorganic — with earths, and salts, and acids, and alkalies — what a glorious dispensation would then dawn upon the world! what transmutations might we then behold, bestowing upon us no longer great accumulation of residuary slag, but, instead thereof, streams of molten gold twice refined!

Did our space permit, it would seem neither an uninteresting nor altogether unprofitable employment to hunt out, and more or less carefully analyze, some of these equivalents we are speaking of. Has it ever occurred to the reader, nay, is there any one to whom it has not occurred, to consider death in this connection — we mean the death of a friend? Who that never lost a friend, especially a very near and dear one, can by any external or substituted apparatus, how ingeniously soever contrived, be put in possession of certain emotions, and thoughts, too, which then flow to us all naturally and spontaneously, when we reach that experience — emotions and thoughts as new and as strange, we had almost said as valuable, as is the gift of sight when first communicated to a blind man? Into what a new world are we not led by this eloquent interpreter — this sharp-eyed, anatomizing revelator — a world otherwise quite beyond our search, or conception even! The traveller in strange latitudes, who is thus made to behold new constellations over his head, gets this privilege, not by telescopes of greater power, but by a change in his position and relations. And so it is with the child of affliction, who, in the very vault of the tomb, all dark and undiademed as it would else be, is made to see stars, and even suns, he had never seen before, nor so much as dreamed of. Among the rest, how idealized has the absent one now become to our imagination, his or her infirmities all forgotten as though they had never been, while the shining qualities are brought out into full relief, and, without help of spiritual or theologic guide, the object of our affection seems enrobed in garments of a lustre and a purity quite dazzling to look upon! And what new "departures" do we not then take — we travellers across this life-ocean — what new estimates, perhaps more correct, too, do we not then form of this mysterious life of ours, now become both more and less mysterious! And while much that once made the greater part of it seems now shrunk and almost vanished away, how do other points that pertain to it loom up into a quite unwonted significance! An equivalent this, it is true, altogether grievous in the payment thereof — more so than any; but we must know that all payments in this kind are for the most part irksome, not for a moment to be brought into comparison with the mere handing over of a certain sum in money, or with the transfer of other chattels and hereditaments, to be on the instant receipted for, and so the debt discharged against us and our heirs forever.

But to return. How inexorable is this law of equivalents in refusing to recognize exchangeable values, we have most notable evidence when it is considered that even wisdom itself, in whose favor we might have supposed an exception would be admissible in this regard, can by no means claim an exemption from its demands. Who more helpless than the scholar is often found to be, outside of his cell? Who oftener falls a prey to quick-scented sharper than the philosopher come down from that upper chamber of his? In our estimate of the author of "The Deserted Village," how much of it goes to admiration of his genius, and how much to pity, if not contempt, for his lack of rugged sense? while even the great lexicographer himself, in whose presence Goldsmith stood overawed, more symmetrically developed as he was, had not always the current coin to save him from certain weaknesses, as we all know; his broad wealth of wisdom standing him in no better stead to protect him against these, than did Baron Rothschild's millions serve to protect him when the inevitable sixpence answered not to his call for omnibus hire. Omnibus charioteer, to be sure, upon learning the quality of his "fare," thus reduced to extremity, avowed his willingness to become his surety for a matter of we know not how many francs; upon which is suggested the pleasing reflection that, upon inquiry therefor, many a laced and scented popinjay would have been forthcoming in the lanes of London to put in pledge his small change, if so be by such offering our ill-provided Samuel Johnson, relieved of his fears of ghosts and hobgoblins, could thus go more freely on his way again. The "inevitable sixpence," we may well suppose, did not very soon fail again to the Baron's call on the streets in Paris: but the "small change" of our popinjay friend — that, we fear, was never at hand; that it never could be reduced into use and possession by him who needed it, we absolutely know.

Under the operation of this law, another principle comes into notice. As we have seen already, the law insists upon, not quantity, but kind. But, even as to kind, it is not always satisfied with a single, homogeneous payment in gross, as of so much gold, but will have a variety of payment, some of which, it often happens, are opposed one to the other, making it difficult for one man to hold them all in possession at the same time. It is under this application of the law that our deepest sympathies are frequently appealed to when our friend or neighbor, having brought the ninety-nine parts of the price, loses the reward because he fails to bring the hundredth; and perhaps we are never made to feel the rigor and severity of the law more than we do in cases of this kind. For it is to be observed that this hundredth part which is withheld is out of all proportion to that which has been paid, not only as to amount, but to our eyes it often seems also quite insignificant, if not absolutely worthless, in kind. Intelligence, sound judgment, strict application to business, prompt integrity, self-denial, — shall these all fail because that seemingly baser coin we denominate impudence was wanting, or because our friend lacked a certain carefulness, or niggardliness of temper, and so did not hoard his gains? The ship thoroughly built with knee-timbers of good royal oak, iron bolts and braces not wanting, all her equipments faultless — shall she founder for that single worm-hole which was overlooked? Shall that single plank, by some oversight not properly fastened, infect and spoil all that prodigality of expenditure? Instances of the kind here alluded to have fallen under the eye of every one, and here, as elsewhere, we lament, and sometimes wonder, that in this individual case the law could not have been suspended, and so our friend have been allowed to get into port with that well-considered enterprise of his.

And the case is still further aggravated when we are made to see how a surplus of price in one kind will by no means excuse payment of all the several kinds. If in trade a man have not gold enough to make this or that purchase, he may possibly eke out the price with some other commodity, and so have his desire. But since this law we are considering knows nothing about barter, recognizes no exchangeable values, surplus in a particular kind goes for nothing. Else how happens it that Robert Burns, and Samuel Taylor Coleridge, and a host of others like them, made in greater or less degree a failure of it? Brain, intellectual force, emotional vigor, too, these men had to a superfluity, so that, if under this law any barter were possible, they might have stood aside for nobody whatever in this world's market.

And, as already intimated, that part of the price which is withheld is often, in our deeming, of very inferior worth, but, for all that, is no less rigidly exacted. In those points where man's nature is most nearly allied to divine, in the loftier gifts of pure intellect, as in the case of Burns and Coleridge just cited, the price is at hand to overflowing, and the failure is to be charged to the absence of certain more sordid and comparatively brutish elements of altogether too despicable a nature to be at all looked after. Upon such nice points as these, however, often turn the scales, and Nature pronounces that an absolute condition which we spurn as beneath our notice.

The subject thus hastily, only suggestively, introduced, admits of wide and varied application. Its special significance is seen in its relation to theories and systems of reform which have for their object the amelioration of man's condition. It invites an examination of these systems and these theories in the light of the law of equivalents. Seeing upon how minute, and to our eyes insignificant, points rests the decision of the question as to success, failure, even in the humblest enterprises, where we might suppose the law would not be always enforced in its full rigor, should there not be hence conveyed to us very emphatic warning lest we overlook and ignore the law in matters of vastly higher moment? May it not possibly be true, nay, is there not very much to give color to the suggestion, that as elsewhere, so here, no barter is admissible? And so, although vast machinery has been got together, and contributions of various kinds have flowed in without stint, until the enterprise has gathered to itself a certain magnificence in the matter of outfit and general appointments, with resources in plenty and to spare, may it not still be true, that it lacks the one essential element of success which, with all its wealth of a different sort, it can in no wise buy, and which it can by no means procure in exchange for some of its superfluous wares? Nay, more: seeing that Nature pronounces that, in certain cases, indispensable which we hold in light esteem, yea, treat with absolute contempt, and that she refuses to recognize a part-payment, however, as to its intrinsic worth incomparably more valuable than that which remains unpaid — is there nothing in all this to put us upon the inquiry as to whether, in great projected reforms, we may not have mistaken altogether the real price, and so have all the time been making offer of something which had no power of temptation whatever?

To illustrate. The unequal distribution of wealth — mere material substance — is in a variety of ways constantly brought under our notice; the poverty, and hence wretchedness, of this man being in strong contrast with the abundance and comfortable life of another. And since to superficial observation and partial analysis of the subject, the only real necessity in the case seems to be to cure this inequality, — to take surplus here and apply it to deficiency there, for men construct railroads, and do a great many other things, on this very simple principle, — the great, almost sole, effort comes to be, to make people give more, that is, more money; so that, material being furnished wherewith to fill up or bridge over these unseemly chasms, the problem is solved; this mere giving we identically pitch upon as the one sole equivalent. If men were less covetous, less selfish, the battle would be as good as won.

But what, in the mean time, becomes of the capacity for receiving? Suppose the selfishness of men were overcome, and their charities greatly multiplied, their personal attention to the proper distribution and application of such charities remaining as it is to-day, and the difficulty of appropriating them on a greatly increased scale without encouraging mendicancy and fraud, and other evils, being still unremoved, what very surprising change for the better could be looked for? It is easy to persuade men to bestow liberally of their substance, for very many motives combine to produce that result. But the sacrifice of their personal ease or convenience, the diligence which is directed to the management of these charitable contributions — how are these to be attained? Of one thing we may be certain: mere money-giving is too cheap and too easy, and the thing itself too base in its nature, ever to be accepted among the higher order of equivalents; nor can it be doubted that the difficulty just alluded to in the way of bestowing extensive charities is intended to teach us the truth of this assertion.

"Let her know her place;
She is the second, not the first."

The above sentiment, which Tennyson has uttered with so much truth in relation to knowledge, may also find application here. Money-giving is the second, not the first. It is an equivalent for very little. Indeed, its highest claim to be reckoned among equivalents at all rests rather upon the reflex influence which it exerts upon the giver himself, or rather, it should be said, upon the influence which it is capable of exerting; for the mere giving, without the emotion, is of no more benefit to the giver than is the paying of a debt, which, in a great many instances, it so closely resembles.

Now, is it not possible that a personal appropriation of these same charities, attended, as it may be, by personal inconvenience, to which, perhaps, we are in the habit of attaching very small value, shall be esteemed that genuine price to which sure reward shall be attached? whereas no return, or at the best a very small one, shall follow upon the more magnificent gift, in the mere bestowing of which we imagine we have nobly discharged our duty, if indeed we do not throw a sop to our pride, and think in our hearts, if we do not utter it with our lips, " What generous men are we ! "

The illustration — for as such, and nothing more, is it here introduced — has somewhat outrun our design. But we would still press the inquiry whether, seeing that in some departments it has been demonstrated to us that failure has resulted from the withholding of what we pronounce a very insignificant, nay, altogether contemptible, part of the price, but which nature declares to be an indispensable part, so that superfluity in some other kind shall in no wise excuse its absence — whether, we say, the same law may not be in force in certain other fields where we have hitherto, to a considerable extent at least, ignored its operation? We think a retrospect of the past history of the race will be found to strengthen the hypothesis here presented. Whenever the world has taken to itself new hope of its own swift-coming regeneration, that hope will be found to have rested almost exclusively upon what may be termed the external "magnificence" of the newly arrived agency; not intending by this word, as here used, mere dazzle, but allowing it to include very much beyond that. The questions for the most part raised respecting this or that enterprise as to its claims upon our confidence — we mean, of course, an enterprise contemplating moral results — have differed very slightly from the questions which arise on the inaugurating of a purely material enterprise. What are its appointments — its available means — its assets? Who are its godfathers? Are they men of large substance, and of acknowledged respectability, both in weight and numbers? Bringing with it what credentials as to its momentum, does this thing now seek introduction to our favor? In a word, is it sufficiently accredited, both as to the extent of the field where it is designed to operate, and as to the machinery it brings with it?

As to all which questions, especially that one of momentum, when has more unequivocally satisfactory answer been rendered than when Johannes Guttenberg, by the art of printing he invented, gave to the world the more rapid mode of diffusing thought? What a gift was there, of a magnificence quite dazzling, as we may suppose, to the recipients, by the verdict of the aggregated wisdom of the world, could it have been assembled, to be exchanged for no gift whatever, if the restoration of a fallen race be the object of attainment! As to which wonderful bestowment, whether it has been doing, or is to-day doing, what was so confidently hoped for from it, answer seems not entirely clear on this day and year of our Lord — certainly not unanimous.

Perhaps the teachings of this law are nowhere more palpably disregarded, and never with more disastrous results, than when men attempt to elevate legislation into the highest place as a remedial, reformatory instrumentality, in those cases where it ought to be held only as subsidiary and contributory. Indeed, it may well be doubted, in view of the mischief which has resulted from an opposite course, whether civil legislation should ever contemplate any direct aid towards a moral enterprise on the ground of its morality. Police regulations derive not their sanctions from, nor do they owe their value to, the fact that they tend to promote virtue. That such encouragement to morality may flow out of such regulations as a collateral result, and that such result may be gratefully accepted, is all true enough. Nay, something more than this may be admitted, and we may conclude that, if no detriment inure to what is the main object in hand, a law may be moulded with a view to such collateral result. If the chief office of government, which is to maintain its own integrity, and to protect its subjects from fraud and violence, be not thus hindered, it would seem only a captious objection, that, in the course of its administration, it encourages virtue in the individual. But that a community should ever be taught, or even suffered to believe, that for any part of the virtue which belongs to it, it is dependent upon a mere legislative act, would be to grievously mistake, or rather to ignore altogether, this law of equivalents. Such payment passes not current at the counter where it is offered. As the coin is itself spurious, so will the thing bargained for prove also spurious. Virtue, in any true sense of the word, is the result of a battle; not to be fought by proxy, not to be conducted by mercenary hirelings, but by the passive endurance, the patient conflict, the bold encounter of the man himself.

And this legislating a people into virtue is only a particular manifestation of a more general error; an error we are always guilty of when we seek to get that by manufacture which is really and only a thing of growth. Everything which lives, which has the principle of life in it, gets its increase by growth, and by growth only. A man may imitate a tree or a fruit. He may manufacture something which externally shall bear a very close resemblance to these objects, even to the point of deceiving the careless beholder; and birds may peck at the simulated grapes on the canvas, as the skill of the celebrated artist has demonstrated. But all the men in the world cannot make a living tree, that shall put forth leaves and bear fruit; and so no more can all the men in the world grow a ship. We may see that the essential conditions of growth are provided; a friendly soil and climate, nutritious food, and protection against enemies. And so much the legislator may do towards promoting virtue in a community. He may by wholesome laws provide the conditions, the external, mechanical aids; but the thing itself he can no more make than he can make a new heaven and a new sun to shine in it.

And so not only of virtue, but of all the moral ingredients which enter into the composition and framework of society, and give us, finally, civilization instead of barbarism; it is still no less true that they come into our hands by a process of growth. Thus it happens that, among others, time comes to be an equivalent for much, nay, for most, that possesses real value, and the impatient reformer who overlooks this condition, and so withholds the price, fails of the reward. His gourd withers with the morning. And perhaps that old fable of Prometheus nowhere finds more fitting application than here. As the crime of which he was guilty well symbolizes their error, who, careless of the conditions, affect to be this world's regenerators, and who thus by implication subject themselves to the charge of attempting to "steal fire from heaven" to get success to their undertakings, so the punishment allotted to him is fit emblem of the gnawing remorse and disappointment which in the end visit these aspiring obstetricians, as they are made finally to contemplate their miserable abortions.

If the gravest complaint against American civilization as it stands typified to-day were to find utterance, it might be resolved into words like these: it tends to one-sidedness in the state — materialism; to many-sidedness in the individuals who compose the state: a condition of things to be so strongly deprecated in both particulars that it is difficult to say which involves the greater injury; a condition of things, too, which, could it only be reversed, making the state many-sided and the citizen one-sided, happiest results might be looked for. Granting, what is doubtless true, that this is an infirmity which belongs intrinsically and always to civilization as such, and so is not peculiar to these times and to these shores, the result is in no wise affected by such consideration. The question still recurs with equal force, how far is the evil susceptible, we will not say of a cure — for that is a word about which hangs a very suspicious odor — but of alleviation? And if we were now attacking a one-sidedness in the state the opposite of that which characterizes the times upon which we have fallen, we should probably find hearers in plenty.

CHAPTER II.

INEXORABLENESS OF THE LAW ILLUSTRATED IN
ITS DEMAND FOR PERSONAL PAYMENT.

THE preceding chapter is in the nature of an introduction, confining itself chiefly to a statement as to what is meant by the Law of Equivalents. The pages which follow will be devoted to illustrating that Law under various heads or subjects; all practical lessons that may be reached, except, indeed, such as flow from a recognition of the law itself, being now held of only secondary importance. Seeking therefore such illustrations as seem best calculated to subserve the main design, I shall not deny myself the use of topics that are hackneyed, nor of thoughts that have long since become the common property of the world. Fully aware that these illustrations must for the most part be drawn from subjects already quite familiar to everybody, I would here disavow, once for all, any claim to freshness or originality; and should a dogmatic form of expression here and there occur in seeming contradiction with this disclaimer, it is hoped the candid reader will not so interpret it.

And nowhere, perhaps, is this disavowal more in place than in speaking, as I now propose to do, of personal labor, of individual effort, as the price, and the sole price, by which certain gifts may become ours. This is a truth which nobody ever thinks of denying. It is so universally admitted, at least speculatively, that any serious argument in its support would be just matter for ridicule. Still, while all this is true, its practical adoption into men's lives is far from having reached perfection, nor can anything which promises to assist towards that result be considered surplusage; so that in this sense the illustration it affords may have a significance beyond the main purpose for which it is introduced, and while it explains what is meant by the Law of Equivalents, may also commend the truth itself to our more hearty adoption. For while there are always obstacles to oppose such adoption, and the disposition generally is to lean upon outside props, I think it will hardly be questioned that there is very much in the type of modern civilization which tends to exalt into unwonted prominence mere external helps, and to induce a reliance upon such helps, even in matters where success is begotten only of that which is personal and internal. The modern systems of education, which go far towards denying the old adage "that there is no royal road to knowledge," and, with pictorial text-books and lessons made easy, would transport the learner with small strain upon his own muscle, illustrate this point. Nor is the explanation far off. The fashion of associated enterprise so prevalent in these days, and the stupendous part machinery is performing for us in the industrial departments, induce a disparaging estimate of personal effort. With so much bestowed upon us, almost as by magic, by extraneous forces, we are prone to forget how much still remains which must be wrought out by us and from us; or, if we do not forget it, we are tempted, under one motive or another, to hope for some compensating substitute for personal labor that shall elevate us to the coveted position. This labor or attention of our own is sometimes irksome, sometimes inconvenient, nay more, is for us sometimes impossible, and we wheedle ourselves into the belief that something else, which we happen to have at hand in copious abundance, will be accepted in its stead. By this solacing expedient we tide ourselves over the difficulty. We find at least temporary relief by the *placebo* thus administered, and hope it "will all come out right in the end." But there is nothing of this kind in store for us. Heaven itself, except by a miracle, cannot bestow upon us that which by the appointment of law is to grow up within us, and that, too, by our own labor.

And how inexorable is this law seen to be in this demand it makes for personal effort! Come bringing in our hands what other price we may, and in what amount soever, it all avails nothing. A penniless beggar, famishing with hunger, might as well hope to purchase a kingdom with the rags that scarce hide his nakedness, as a man to convert to his own use another's experience, or to receive at the hands of others what Nature has foreordained must flow out of his own life. Patience, for instance, humble as is the rank it is often made to hold in the catalogue of virtues, is not infrequently coveted by a man whose rashness of conduct or precipitancy of temper has brought trouble upon him. But can he get it in a day by any force of high resolve, by any strong endeavor? Were he ready to cut off his right hand, or to pluck out his right eye, so that this quality might become his own, — would such sacrifice bestow it upon him? In the whole list of his possessions and resources, money, friends, wit, a powerful intellect, ardent emotion, an active imagination, or what not, — is there any one of them he can part with and have this in return? Not one. Not all of them united can buy it for him; but there are men all around him who, never having had his various wealth, still have this element.

Self-respect — men are often made to see its value, and what advantages it brings with it. They are made to observe the superiority of the man who has it over the man who has it not, and they earnestly desire to become themselves possessors of it, if for no other reason, at least for the fruits that it yields. And can he have his desire, — this man who has never paid the price? Never, until the price be paid. The united wealth of the world, and the united efforts of all the men in the world, nay, Omnipotence itself, cannot bestow it upon him. "Pay me the price," "Hand over to me the equivalent," is Nature's unrelenting demand, and then the thing you desire will happen to you without demand of yours. It comes to you; you have no need to go for it.

So I might go on to enumerate other qualities, each in like manner to be had on similar terms. But a more general application is furnished by the subject of education. Estimated in the light of this law we are considering, how much is uttered on that topic which is quite wide of the mark! Take, for instance, the labored arguments in relation to the study of the "dead languages," so called. The most popular objection urged against them as part of a collegiate course is, that they are not of practical use. This, indeed, is very far from being true, even in the inferior sense intended by those who make use of it. But just now I let that pass, only remarking that, although a knowledge of them does not help a man to draw water, or to hew wood, or to build ships, it does help the man who uses, not an axe, but language, as an instrument; and inasmuch as language is our medium of thought, and thought moves the world, it would not seem to be so destitute even of "practical" value as these its opponents contend.

But whether or not any practical value attends their study, depends upon the answer which this question receives: What is man? If he is only a calculating machine, a little improved upon that constructed by the ingenious Mr. Babbage; if the machine be simple and not complex, and so have but one set of wants and but one thing to do, — then not only these dead languages, but very much that is now preserved in our own living language, may have leave to take themselves out of the way with all possible dispatch. For the argument which would banish Greek and Latin from our schools and our colleges, if consistent, must also banish English, that is, a large portion of it, from our libraries and our families. Of what possible practical use, pray, are Charles Lamb's "Essays," or Shakespeare's "Tempest," or "Hamlet," or "Midsummer Night's Dream," or Milton's "Comus," or "Paradise Lost," or Tennyson's "In Memoriam"? Of what practical value are the creations of Scott, or Bulwer, or Thackeray, or Charlotte Brontë, or of their illustrious compeer whose untimely decease the world has not done wearing sackcloth for to-day? Of what practical use is any book, or any study, Greek, Latin, or English, unless it be an arithmetic or an algebra?

But unfortunately for the argument, though fortunately for the world, man is not a mere calculating machine; his mechanism is not simple, but complex; his wants are not few, but many; he has not one thing, but many things to do. And this being true, he must make payment of something besides money, or even algebra; and to do this, he must receive something besides money, or what breeds money. He must be prepared to make variety of payment, for this is the law of equivalents; and from its inexorableness it follows, as just barely possible, that the study of these "dead" languages is of identically the most practical value of all studies whatever. It is barely possible that this complex mechanism has wants to be supplied, and duties to be performed, both of which demands are met by that identical operation and discipline which is furnished by this identical study. And were this the proper place, I think it might be demonstrated that there is no disciplinary mental process whatever which in so broad and various a sense furnishes "equivalents," in a system of general education, as precisely this one furnishes them. Nor will this law be found a single whit less inexorable here than elsewhere. The man shall have his choice, but having made it, and elected one supreme object of desire, he shall never be allowed to amend his prayer, and so by circumventing Nature by some trick or stratagem, or by propitiating her by some illegitimate costly sacrifice, receive in the end what in the beginning he refused to pay for.

Nor perhaps do men who thus hope to receive a double reward in return for a single price, have it in mind either to cajole Nature into compliance with their demands by bribery, or to overcome her by artifice. The cheat is one they rather practise upon themselves, and by an excess of misapplied labor — by what they consider a magnanimous overdoing in a certain direction which is demonstrably wrong, but which is easy and palatable to them; by, as it were, doing a sort of penance by superfluous contributions, and so making requital for their delinquency by some such atoning process not wearing very distinct shape even in their own minds — they hope the scales will turn in their favor at last. Woful, fatal mistake! This law will have its dues, not only to the uttermost farthing, but it will have them in kind. It knows nothing about recompense to be made in some other commodity, — nothing about bills of accommodation, — nothing about suretyship, or payment to be made by another. With a more than Shylock inexorableness, it insists upon the bond, aye, upon its very letter, — the pound of flesh, and that to be cut from nearest to the heart; all intercessions, all contributions from imploring friends, being to it vain and idle as the passing wind.

But the assumption seems almost if not quite universal, that, in all cases where extraordinary exertion is used, great expenditure resorted to, and vast machinery set in motion, some advance must be made irrespective of any effort on the part of the individual. Here is a community, we will suppose, bountifully supplied with all these outside helps and incentives, libraries open to all, free lectures, churches thronged, schools through the week and on the Sabbath. I do not mean certainly that these are without value. I do not mean that they are not serviceable aids in the promotion of virtue and order. They doubtless are, and it is only reasonable to expect to find a community like that described far in advance of one which does not enjoy these privileges. But they operate indirectly. They do not reach the dignity of equivalents. All put together they neither do nor can in themselves bestow upon a single individual in that community any real virtuous principle,— an assertion which, if it were doubted, might easily be confirmed by separating such individual from these external influences, and transporting him to a spot where he should encounter opposite influences. Under such a change this mere external virtue falls away from him. It was all the time only spurious, for a spurious price had been paid for it. Hence there is really nothing wonderful in the fact that such a man, in spite of all these " advantages," makes a wreck of himself at last; and the surprise often expressed by very good people, who cannot understand how this or that one who has come under their observation should turn out so badly, is really without any just grounds. He never paid the price, and where is the cause for either complaint or wonder that he failed of the reward?

The real ground of wonder is, that the same persons who receive this law in their daily business, and so far as their material interests are concerned govern their actions by it, think to escape its operation in the moral world. Men do not, for the most part, locate cities in this way. They do not build houses and stores, and palatial hotels with marble or brown-stone fronts, on the supposition that these, with whatever excess of outlay and gorgeous appointments, will atone for the absence of natural advantages. They know very well that this mere excess of expenditure will not of itself attract trade, — that it will not make a city. I do not mean that they never, nor in any degree, overlook this law, even in these matters. They sometimes fall into errors of judgment on these points; and altogether a disagreeable object to look upon is, for instance, an overgrown hotel, called somebody's "Folly," and properly too, since, wrongly located, the best thing it could ever get done for itself was to put out its fires, shut up its doors and windows, and go as fast as possible into decay and forgetfulness, — no noise of wheels, or winter bells, or horses champing their bits at the door; no boisterous hostlers running to and fro; no ruddy-faced, cheerful landlord; no merry housemaid chucked under the chin in the long passages; no patter-patter of slipper of gentle dame adown the staircases; but instead of these a miserable discord of discontented shutters, sole accompaniment to the forlorn signboard which creaks in the gusty wind, altogether a fit emblem of another "Folly" which, in the ordering and the locating of moral enterprises, gives no heed to the law of equivalents.

But to return to our illustration from education. Remote allusion has been made already to the prevalent fashion of introducing the labor-saving principle into this department. Labor-saving machinery appears to be most advantageously resorted to in all the so-called industrial pursuits. In the long run it cheapens many products, thus bringing them within reach of a larger class, and so adding not only to their physical comfort, but also elevating them morally, since, as a general rule, we never make men more comfortable without at the same time making them better. Indeed, if the admission did not imply something a little humiliating to our vanity, we should be found perhaps attributing more efficacy to this instrument of moral advancement than we now seem inclined to do. But letting this pass, the disposition manifests itself on every side to appropriate this principle to systems of education. There are, for instance, contrivances for rapidly filling storehouses with grain; why not, by some equally commodious and rapid process, fill the mind with facts? Elsewhere there are swift modes of conveyance and transfer: why not convey and transfer knowledge to the ignorant by a similar happy arrangement?

Now it is evident to everybody who has bestowed a moment's thought upon the subject, that the labor-saving principle applied to education involves several fallacies, only a few of which can be noticed here. And perhaps the greatest of them all is that which assumes that the bestowing of knowledge, the acquisition of facts, is education. It is doubtless true that, in the process of being educated, men do acquire knowledge. They are conducted to the possession of facts to which they were formerly strangers. But this only happens to be so, and if some other method of education could be devised better calculated to accomplish its purpose, and so no new facts or knowledge be acquired at all, such method would be entitled to precedence over the present existing one.

And this is true for a twofold reason. First, mere facts, or the knowledge of them, are not, in the strict sense of the term, equivalents. The oft-quoted aphorism of Bacon, that "knowledge is power," is true only in a qualified sense. Magliabecchi, the librarian, was a man of wonderful learning, but he was little more than a receptacle of it under a somewhat different form from the shelves in the alcoves over which he presided. Neither, for all his knowledge, was he necessarily an "educated" man, whatever the fact may have been. But the remark is too evidently and palpably true to need to be fortified by argument here. Some of the most helpless men we ever meet with are learned men. They may form — they doubtless do form — exceptions to the general rule, for the mere process of acquiring knowledge has, *virtute officio,* a tendency at the same time to educate the faculties that are employed in such process. All I here assert is, that there is no necessity that should be so. A man may have great store of knowledge, and be only imperfectly educated; he may have little knowledge, and be well educated.

And it is the education of the faculties, not the knowledge acquired in the course of the process, that constitutes an equivalent. All contrivance after the fashion of grain-elevators, all swift and easy modes of conveyance and transfer of bulk, seem not quite up to the mark. The mere acquisition of facts is not education, nor are the two things necessarily connected. Knowledge, facts, are rather the tools which the workman uses, and education is that process by which he learns how to use them effectively. But a skilful workman with few tools has the advantage of the awkward workman with many tools. Skill is better than knowledge. It has inherent dignity, inherent power. It is, in a word, an equivalent.

But, however mere knowledge may be conveyed to us by a sort of mechanical process, this skill I speak of comes to us by no such channel. It is the result of personal effort, of our own individual industry. It includes many things, — a power of concentration, of analysis, of discrimination, habits of prolonged and steady application, and much else. But these were never conferred upon a man from without. The father who thinks to appoint a certain lot for his son, who without stint of money procures for him "all the advantages," flattering himself the while that this object of his care shall thereby grow up to be a glory to himself, and an honor and ornament to his friends, does at the best furnish the occasion under which these results may happen; the pregnant cause of them lying many thousands of miles beyond reach of his.

But we must not tarry. The foregoing remarks introduce the second reason for the assertion that education does not consist in the acquisition of facts, and therefore is not a mechanical process to be compassed by labor-saving machinery. The first reason, as we have just seen, is, that knowledge is in itself barren. To make it effective, either for the edification of the subject of it, or for the producing of external results, it must be associated with skill, and all that skill includes. But this skill is the result of the very labor which it is proposed to avoid. It is in the very act of laboring that those mental habits, and those intellectual forces already alluded to, come into our hands. And they come to us in no other way. Discipline, development, training, or what other synonym soever we employ, means labor — labor of the man himself. And could we suppose such a thing were possible, and an invention should be placed in our hands by which knowledge should be conveyed to us like a piece of merchandise, the man who should bestow such an invention upon the world would be its greatest enemy if, by the terms of it, it should dispense with labor on our part. For just as we are made perfect through suffering as to our moral nature, and by passing through the low grounds of affliction, nay, almost of despair, we are at last borne to heights we could never otherwise have attained; just as in the school of adversity we receive lessons we could have learned nowhere else, — so there is but one way possible in which the intellect may reach its utmost perfection, and that is, its own exercise. That result happens to us, not by accident, nor by gift, nor by purchase, nor by inheritance, nor by finding, nor by prayer, even though that prayer ascend from a mother's heart; neither by any external help of curiously contrived text-book; but it is conveyed to us, if at all, by the one single channel of our own individual effort.

And the thoughts, or facts rather, here reproduced, so at once familiar and incontestable, attest what I have been attempting to illustrate, — that the Law of Equivalents is an inexorable law. As we cannot recall a single exception to it in all the past, so we feel quite certain that the future will unfold a similar record.

CHAPTER III.

INEXORABLENESS OF THE LAW ILLUSTRATED IN ITS REFUSING TO RECOGNIZE CLAIMS FOUNDED ON THE COMMENDABLE CHARACTER OF THE ENTERPRISE.

In the views I am attempting to unfold, it has been assumed that romance is characteristic of the American mind in an eminent degree. It has been asserted that, in the pursuit of a certain class of objects, it casts itself loose from law, and, without any sufficient guaranty therefor, amuses itself with the expectation of certain magnificent results in the spiritual world, somewhat proportioned to those which have been reached in the material universe; and I shall attempt hereafter to find partial explanation of this fact in certain external circumstances of unwonted splendor that have attended the development of American civilization in its purely physical aspects, whose contagious influence has reached over into other departments.

There is, however, another exhibition of this romantic element not referable to this source, and not confined to the American people, but still belonging to them in a very marked degree. And it is this: the commendable character of an enterprise, and the lofty ends it proposes, are supposed to relieve it in some sort from the rigorous demands of law, and by force of something that is not law, but accident,— by some fortuitous event, or some exceptional interposition in its behalf, which still shall not reach the dignity of a miracle, — it is to attain a fortunate issue. To judge from their actions, there would seem to be very many who refuse to believe that a good cause can ever have bad measures enlisted in its support; or in other words, the cause being good, whatever is offered in its behalf will be sanctified and overruled for the advantage of such cause. No reasoning in its support can be unsound, no argument be false.

And perhaps the Law of Equivalents is never so summarily disposed of as it is in those instances where the commendable character of the movement is supposed to imply a relaxation or suspension of law in its favor. There are vast numbers whom it would be very difficult indeed to make believe that in this particular, that is, the favor with which they are regarded by law, good and bad enterprises stand upon precisely the same level. With them, very frequently the strongest argument of all for believing in the success of an enterprise, as well as for espousing every measure that professes to assist it, is the unexceptionable aim it proposes. They seem to suppose that, while law will always govern in matters of comparative insignificance, and inferior value, and questionable propriety, in matters of trade, buying and selling, building ships and houses, the moment man leaves these more grovelling pursuits, and bends his energies and directs his self-sacrifice to something higher,— to the advancement of his fellow-men and the amelioration of their condition, — Nature will abate something of her rigor, and, taking into account their extraordinary zeal and costly efforts, will, as it were, meet them half-way. They are conscious how they are themselves influenced, and not improperly, by such considerations. They often reward good intentions, even though they be attended by unwise and insufficient measures. The father does not always insist upon success in his child, nor upon unerring judgment. He rewards the effort, especially if it be honest. The employer, sometimes at least, pays wages that have not been earned by any return that came, or could come, to himself. And why should not Nature be equally supple and accommodating? Why should not Nature, out of that bountiful hand of hers, apportion her gifts to the purity of the motive, and the costliness of the sacrifice, and the magnificence of the gift, and not always insist upon our approaching her by this or that particular avenue, and bringing in our hands this or that particular offering?

And the solicitations with which, under the romantic assumption above indicated, they approach Nature, are mainly two: first, excess or superfluity of payment; and then, substitution. Even should they have reached this point of discovery,— that absolutely gratuitous favors are not to be expected, even in behalf of praiseworthy undertakings, they still hope to evade the specific payment by works of supererogation, or by substituting something else, which, being in their estimation of equal value, or demanding from them an equal sacrifice, they imagine must have an equal power of temptation. We find a popular illustration of this weakness in the ranting declaimer who, by boisterousness of manner, vehemence of gesture, and impassioned utterance, strives to atone for the lack of higher qualities. The religious zealot, who seeks to propagate his sentiments by the sword and the fagot; the reformers in social science, who resort to mere statutory enactments to effect the change they contemplate; the political philosophers, who think by a change in the form of government, and by the introduction of free institutions, to bestow the blessings of liberty,— all these afford illustrations to the same purpose.

But these men are not always dishonest or selfish men. The fanatics who kindled the fires of the Spanish Inquisition were not always cruel men, thirsting for the blood of their victims. They were not always and only stimulated by love of power and glory to the extreme measures they adopted. The testimony is abundant to prove that they were frequently men of tender emotions, who thought to save errorists from eternal fires by the flames they were exposed to on earth. Their own error was in believing that force could be converted into an instrument that should affect men's belief. They failed to recognize the Law of Equivalents. They attempted a substituted price for the real one. They succeeded in some instances in extorting an outward compliance. But all the hideous spectacle presented to us in the annals of those times, all the sufferings of the agonized victims as their souls were released from their tortured bodies, was not the price of a single honest conversion to the prescribed faith.

Attempts at social reform are still further to the same purpose. The history of sumptuary laws, the elaborately devised schemes of Fourier, and others his inferiors, who with like purpose and like failure have succeeded him, owe their origin to the same source. This field, indeed, has furnished signal illustration in point, not only attracting experimenters in past ages, but down to the present hour it seems to have lost none of its seductiveness. Its own vastness, and the vast fruits it seems capable of yielding, constantly invite new theories and speculations. It offers a temptation to uneasy innovators inferior only to that which instigated the religious persecutions above noticed of a former period; the magnitude of the evils proposed to be removed affording now, as then, apology for excesses which would not otherwise be tolerated. As the actors in those scenes, from which we proudly fancy ourselves separated as much by principle and by sentiment as we are by time, — scenes whose mere recital thrills our souls with horror, — justified themselves to the world and to their own consciences as the saviors of their victims from eternal punishment, so these modern manipulators point in justification of their excesses to results which they contemplate; so they establish themselves in transient favor with the public they succeed in cajoling with their promises.

But, themselves often the victims of romantic sentiments, it affords little cause of wonder that they should infect their credulous dupes with a similar weakness. The field they have selected for their operations is not only vast, but the objects it includes are numerous as intricate, intricate as momentous. The laws that pertain to them are laws of life, of health, of growth, of development, and they are thus, in the very nature of the case, involved in mystery and uncertainty. The twilight obscurity which invests this class of subjects, their vagueness of outline, the long and tortuous and mysteriously dark passages by which they are approached, and through which the expedition is to be conducted, are altogether favorable to romantic estimates and chimerical hopes; while disgrace of oft-reiterated discomfiture is easily turned away from the performers for the same reasons. Failure itself, on a stage of such huge proportions, brings renown, or at least notoriety, which success in inferior fields never bestows. "Hero" and "martyr" are words almost consecrated to these modern alchemists, who, unlike their great prototypes, generally manage to keep back from the crucible, where the experiment goes on, their own possessions, and put to venture the interests of their neighbors only.

The same romantic habit of reasoning, if reasoning it can be called, finds constant illustration, on a broader scale, in our estimates of national strength and solidity, and in the balancing of our own chances, as compared with other nations, for a long life and an ever-increasing prosperity. The free institutions we have adopted, contrasting so strongly with the despotic rule of other lands; the claim we set up as offering an asylum for the oppressed; the whole theory of the government, supposed to be in favor of right, of justice, of equality, of protection for all and a fair chance for every man, — all this gives us an exalted idea of our superiority; and in close connection follows the belief that Heaven regards the experiment with complacency, and that in some way or other exceptional interposition will be made in our behalf. There were probably many thousands who, before the late disastrous civil war, firmly believed it was impossible, upon no better grounds than these. Indeed, it has been the practice of certain religious teachers for many years, to assume for what special purpose Providence reserved this continent; and whatever seemed likely to obstruct such purpose thus by them divined, they believed themselves, and taught others to believe, could never happen. Of this, however, I shall remark in another place.

And in spite of the terrible lesson just alluded to, had by us at so fearful a cost, there are vast numbers to-day who believe that Heaven regards the American people, and the experiment they are putting to the test, with such approbation that general laws will be, if not absolutely suspended, at least relaxed, rather than such experiment should fail. But they at the same time would spurn the imputation, should they be charged with looking for a miracle. Many of them do not believe in miracles, past or present, but this fancy of theirs must be brought about somehow or other, else — the hopes of the world will be disappointed.

But unless the whole doctrine of the Law of Equivalents be false, the American system must take its chance with all other systems. However there may belong to it any real or supposed fitness to promote virtue or the happiness of its subjects, it can claim no exemption from the common lot. When it offers Equivalents, it will receive the rewards that are attached to such Equivalents. Admitting it to possess all the excellent qualities that its fondest admirers ever claimed for it, and bringing it into comparison with that system which is most opposed to it, there is no reason to expect supernatural intervention, in one case more than in the other, to mitigate the consequences of transgression, or to supply the remedy for an omission. The responsibility and the operative agency of man are not to be thus easily eliminated from the great problem of civilization. Human laws may take into consideration human weaknesses, and may to a certain extent accommodate themselves to exceptional cases; but even these have a uniformity belonging to them, so that in their individual application they work sometimes harshly, if not unjustly. But the great general laws by which the universe is controlled know nothing of exceptional cases. The winds of heaven will blow in the same direction, whether the effect be favorable or adverse to a right enterprise. They may bring the missionary who bears the gospel to heathen lands a victim to the bloody pirate who scours the seas in search of booty, or they may carry him to safety in an opposite direction; but they will not know or consider which is the missionary, nor who or what is his foe.

Now in these instances above cited, and in a vast multitude of similar ones, the attempt is to get something which must be paid for in kind, and to substitute some other than the one sole appointed price. It is to climb over into the fold by some surreptitious contrivance of our own, — a contrivance recommended to us, perhaps, as being easier, perhaps as reflecting credit upon ourselves, perhaps as flattering to our vanity. And the plea we offer why we should be indulged in this substitution is, that our motives are good, our enterprise is a commendable one. It will help the needy, it will fortify us against temptation, it will lessen crime, it will promote virtue, in various ways it will add to the happiness of men and to the wellbeing of society. The secret hope of our hearts is, that " under the circumstances " Nature will be cajoled into a compliant mood by the costliness of our offering, — that Heaven will be at last overcome by the importunity of our prayers. Thus, under the seductive lure of romance, we wander into barren paths; thus by a sickly sentimentality our energies corrode, and life exhausts itself in impotent longings and fruitless enterprises.

But I must remind the reader once more, that the plan of this treatise allows little else than a bald statement, and does not profess to follow out any single thought or topic into its various and ramified relations. The great variety of subjects introduced evidently forbids any such attempt, unless the book were swollen into proportions quite beyond the author's design.

On the point we have just been considering, I therefore here bring my remarks to a close, only adding, that those who hope to escape from this

Law of Equivalents, because their enterprise is a commendable one, can do so only upon terms of disturbing and overthrowing the very constitution of the moral universe. For this is just what an Equivalent means. This law is something established by Nature, or rather is only a statement of what Nature is. It is not a mere arbitrary rule like that which a man may establish and withdraw capriciously and at his pleasure; and instead of saying, as we do of a man who is inexorable, that he will not yield, it would be more proper to say of this law that it cannot yield. It is inexorable because it has no power of being anything else. It is part and parcel of the great general economy of the universe, which has determined unalterably the office of every element, and the relation which each element shall severally bear to every other, equivalents being fixed in the moral world with the same certainty that belongs to them in the material world. A certain degree of cold, or absence of heat, is necessary to convert water into ice. Such result can be reached in no other way, but it happens itself, if the expression is admissible, upon the conditions being supplied; nor can the wit of man prevent its happening, or by any application of force prevent its happening, according to the laws which govern the process, and so increase its bulk. The healing art, perhaps, furnishes a more significant illustration. The practitioner has frequent occasion to administer a stimulant, in order that the patient's vital force shall not be exhausted before the applied remedial agents produce the desired result. He can kill the disease, if the patient will only live long enough. And this point he can manage if he can only avail himself of the power for good which the stimulant supplies, and at the same time avoid its capacity for evil. But can he do this? Can he thus divide and separate its powers? His purpose is a benevolent one, his motive good; and will not this stimulant, so indispensably necessary to keep the patient along, for once consent to be something else than it is, — that is to say, give strength, and yet not impart heat or a quicker flow to the blood? The question answers itself. The stimulant has its own properties which make it an Equivalent for a certain result, and upon its "exhibition" those results happen, but they cannot be divided.

CHAPTER IV.

SAME THOUGHT PURSUED IN SPEAKING OF RO-
MANCE AS INFECTING THEOLOGY.

ANY doubt that may have disturbed the reader, as to what was intended by imputing romance to the American mind, has probably been dissipated by the preceding chapter. Intimately connected with the topic there discussed, is a certain favorite hypothesis, which, indebted perhaps for its origin to the American pulpit, has come at last to hold a quite prominent place in the hearts of the people at large.

In years past it has been by no means an unusual thing to hear from the sacred desk words like these: "This continent has been reserved by the Almighty Ruler of the universe for the special manifestation of his power and glory. By his immutable decree, civil and religious liberty are here to find a home of assured safety,— a field of operation which shall yield triumphs hitherto unknown. The Church, as his accredited agent, is here to be signalized by victories far exceeding anything hitherto witnessed."

Such have been the utterances of men, claiming to be only men, who, unable to resist the force of the current in its fervid sweep, have been borne away victims to that extravagant temper it should have been their aim to hold in check. The very boldness of the predictions unwarranted by anything but an overheated imagination or an ardent fancy, ought to have made us fear lest they should share the fate of similar vaticinations in the past. But they were offered to ears all ready and willing to receive them, and it is doubtful if the history of the world affords a more remarkable instance of romantic speculation and sublime imaginings, having for their foundation nothing but the accidents of the hour.

Indeed, there was very much to give logical contradiction to such pleasing assurances. No new spiritual aids were placed in our hands by the discovery and settlement of the new continent. On the contrary, immense additional incentives were thus furnished to a purely material progress. The Equivalents thus acquired by us were of the kind which produce a secular growth and prosperity, and which are calculated to stimulate great industrial enterprises, whose result is to produce wealth,— to amass in abundance the perishable products of earth. The new theatre thus opened up for the exhibition of human energy was surely not one we should have naturally selected as favorable to high religious culture,— to any extraordinary attainments in spiritual life. That presupposes certain habits of thought and certain experiences quite the opposite of those which were likely to arise where men constantly encountered on every side so much to minister to their egoism and self-adulation, — so much to flatter their vanity and keep alive a sense of independence.

It would seem, too, that it might have been partially conjectured, if not clearly foreseen, that mechanism, in the unfolding of the great drama, would have anything but a spiritualizing tendency. If not already developed into actual existence, it was among the strongly suggested possibilities of the future, and so might have imposed a slight check upon our imaginations. A supernatural interposition doubtless might mitigate and even neutralize the effect of these hostile forces. And were there any reason to expect aid of this nature, mere logical conclusions might be set aside as irrelevant. But even assuming that the designs of the great Ruler of the universe are capable of being penetrated by human vision; assuming that the intentions attributed to Him in regard to the newly discovered continent, and the people who were to occupy it, were rightly interpreted, and that the principles and motives by which such people were to be actuated had his approbation; there was no warrant for expecting any such miraculous interference. The historical proof is ample and indisputable on this point. Over and over again, in the struggle between true and false systems, has occurred the fit opportunity, judged by man's wisdom, for the special exercise of divine power. Over and over again the speedy exercise of such power has been predicted as sure to happen; and from the falsification of such predictions, over and over again, distrust and scepticism have been begotten. The time has been when men sought to avert physical suffering by propitiating the God or Gods of their worship, so that the pestilence might be stayed on its errand of death; that the destructive force of the hurricane or the volcano might be arrested; that plenty might take the place of wasting famine; and perhaps such sentiments hold their place in many hearts to-day. But those who watch more closely the undeviating operation of law, have long since dismissed such expectations as altogether unwarrantable.

Nor is there any reason to suppose that a different rule obtains in the spiritual and moral world. Bad enterprises succeed, good enterprises fail, according as they are affected by the laws which belong to them. Bad men often prosper, good men are often overtaken by adversity; and any argument in favor of virtue and against vice based upon reward in this world for one, and punishment in this world for the other, is felt at once and by everybody to be not only unsound but mischievous, since we are no sooner taught that such distinction may be expected than, upon the disappointment which is sure to ensue, our faith receives a shock nearly or quite fatal.

Any supernatural intervention, then, to cure the mechanical tendency just alluded to, was, plainly enough, not to be counted upon. The type of civilization for us was to be the unheroic, the unimaginative, the unimpressible. How this has come to be the prevailing type to-day, is plain to the most careless inspection. It reigns in every heart — over every man's life. Egoist as he is under so many combined influences, political, climatic, and physical, and holding fast to his individualism in the estimates he forms of himself, his rights, and his prerogatives, he by a singular contradiction fails to understand how this individual life and character of his are of specific value to the commonwealth and to society. These, forsooth, live upon quite a different aliment. For himself, he is a self-worshipper: looking upon himself as of any account to the state, he is a self-immolator, not indeed sacrificing himself as did Curtius by leaping into the chasm that threatened to ingulf Rome, but denying, practically at least, that he possesses any value in that regard. He must associate himself with some one or more of the organizations of the day, and so get to himself the advantage which machinery bestows everywhere. For society never so abounded in these separate organized companies as to-day,— ring-fences, as De Quincey calls them, within whose sacred pale cliques and sub-cliques disport themselves withal, excluding as contraband whatever bears not the mystic badge, the true ear-mark. He believes in numerical value and in statistical tables, because most values he is familiar with are estimated in that way. Enrolled on the list of consecrated worthies who have organized a special advocacy for this or that object, he feels that he has added a cubit to his stature. If he does not weigh more, he counts more.

And so everywhere. Machinery is the philosopher's stone. It even builds churches, and very much after the same fashion that it builds factories and steamboats. We do not, it is true, yet hear a church described as of so many horse-power, but we are very often advertised as to the sum-total of expenditure, what rent-roll the pews produce, what is the capacity for holding, and how many are the believers; how much the belief, whether it be more or less than fell to the lot of a single monk in the olden times, not being always quite so carefully ascertained.

And it were by no means either uninteresting, nor altogether uninstructive, to attempt to-day what was due to a former period, but was then omitted; and by applying these suggestions to the present existing situation; that is, by discarding romance and accepting logic; derive what profit from them they may have it in their power to bestow. The cloud in the political future, even if it be no bigger than a man's hand, is none the less a cloud, nor can it become less by any romantic speculation we may choose to indulge in. There are two elements at work in American civilization quite as antipodal each to the other — quite as sensitive and combustible in their nature, and pregnant with quite as important consequences, as were the other two, Liberty and Slavery, whose opposite claims have only just now terminated in the convulsions of civil war. On this day and year of our Lord, the Protestant feels secure. "Plymouth Rock," the "Puritan Fathers," "Spanish Inquisition,"— these, and other similar words and expressions, are on our lips with a certain supposed power of incantation which shall save us unscathed. But the days of witches and witchcraft are over, at least, it may be hoped, for the present generation. The only incantation possible for us is that which reason, not sentiment, shall afford. Whatever be the enterprise we are contemplating with a view to horoscopic results, we must survey it in its logical aspects, if we desire to be conducted to a safe conclusion. Dreams, even if they be day-dreams, will not answer. Visions, be they of what surpassing beauty and excellence soever, will melt and vanish away, as it is the nature of visions to do. The man, any number of men acting in concert, who come bringing with them the Equivalent, it matters not what may be the good or the bad, the wholesome or the unwholesome character of the enterprise in hand, will receive the reward.

It will be understood at once that, as to the claims which Protestantism and Romanism severally put forth, I have here and now nothing to say. Nor is it necessary to my present purpose to go into any inquiry of the sort. Whether one or both, or one more than the other, is to be regarded as a mere ambitious sect, bent upon making proselytes and so extending and assuring its power, — whether one is a pure gospel of truth revealed from heaven, and the other Anti-Christ, — has nothing to do with what I am now endeavoring to illustrate. They must both encounter law. They must each of them acquire victory or sustain defeat as they adapt or not their movements to the requisitions of law. They must each of them bring Equivalents, or they will return empty-handed.

And sitting in judgment upon these two hostile forces, banishing all thought of their respective merits as having neither part nor lot in the matter, which of the twain to-day are most palpably doing this? Observing them, taking note of their movements as we would do if we had under our eye only a mere secular enterprise which was aiming at only secular results, what must be the impartial judgment? I enter into no conjecture as to which in our estimation is best entitled to a relaxation or suspension of law to cure its mistakes or atone for its omissions, because I believe neither will be permitted to avail itself of any such exceptional intervention.

And having premised so much, I am constrained to say that the Romanist has the advantage. But even if this were demonstrably true, which many persons taking counsel of their emotions will straightway deny, it were of small avail to announce it unless there were some hope of a remedy. The question, then, returns, — If the Romanist has the advantage, wherein does it consist? And I think mainly here. He never relaxes exertion in the expectation of receiving aid from Heaven to atone for his own delinquencies. He runs his whole machinery, if I may be allowed the expression, as he would run a purely secular enterprise. He omits no duty, he abates nothing of energy, in the hope that a higher power will supply the omission. He is emphatically a hard worker. His doctrine, and his practice too, is to achieve what he can with his own hands, accepting thankfully whatever else may be added thereto. And more particularly, he admits no schism. He fights, as Napoleon did, by concentrating his forces, not scattering them. His opponent rather professes indifference as to schism, finds a stimulant in it, or some other advantage. In the multiplication of sects he finds pleasing evidence of a critical, inquisitive spirit, altogether in very strong contrast with the more stagnant, docile, and obedient temper of the Romanist. Certainly. Who questions all this? But what then? Shall divided ranks succeed against those which are united? While this active, schismatic spirit of intelligence amuses itself with attacks upon its friends, — the Methodist, the Baptist, the Congregationalist, the Presbyterian, and other Christian denominations, carrying on a sort of guerrilla warfare among themselves, wasting their ammunition in their own camp, — is the more compact front which the adversary presents to be stripped of the advantage such union affords, merely because the aforesaid Christian sects are after all in the main at one, their want of harmony being only apparent, and not real? It may be true that their agreement is greater than their disagreement. The distinctions which divide them into separate sects may be quite insignificant, compared with the opposition which possesses them towards their common foe; but they nevertheless make void a united opposition. Judged, therefore, by any rules applicable to secular matters, the two opposing parties exhibit in this particular very unequal degrees of skill; and I am not sure but the sentiment finds as appropriate application here as anywhere, which declares that the " children of this world are wiser in their generation than the children of light."

Romanism, Protestantism, — what a volume do these words include! As through long centuries they have each struggled for the mastery, what fierce conflicts, what bloody battle-fields, what persecutions, what fluctuating fortunes, what depositions of rulers, what risings of an exasperated populace, what burnings at slow fires, what secret conclaves of ambitious conspirators, what boldness of reformers, what jesuitical craft, what sundering of families, what disruption of kingdoms, what edicts of councils, what St. Bartholomew massacres, rise in long succession before the eye of the observer! — a tumultuous assemblage, where, in apparently chaotic confusion, to quote the lines of the Latin poet, —

> Frigida pugnabant calidis, humentia siccis,
> Mollia cum duris, sine pondere habentia pondus.

But can it be for a moment questioned, that throughout all the alternating successes and disasters which have from time to time attended the march of these two antagonistic forces, — that while victory seems now inclined to perch upon these standards and now upon those, — can it be questioned that law has ever maintained her supremacy? And if we accept the theory of undeviating law as applicable, the explanation of these alternating successes and discomfitures is easy and simple enough. For in that case the capriciousness and the infirmities of man account for the irregular and capricious results. A necessary uniformity belonging to law, and a capricious temper belonging to man, irregular and inconsequent results were evidently to be looked for; and if the cause of truth and virtue has sometimes failed, and error and vice have triumphed, this cannot be taken as evidence that the former is not superior to the latter. But if we suppose some other power than law, and therefore a power under no necessity to act with uniformity; and something else than man, and therefore under no temptation to act capriciously, — if we suppose some such power has had the control, so that nothing prevented the order of affairs from being conducted more in accordance with what seemed the proprieties of the case, we cannot avoid asking why the exercise of such a power should not have been uniformly and always had in favor of that which we pronounce right? If intervention be not impossible in the very nature of the case, and still more, if it be claimed as sometimes actually happening, but in the majority of cases be withheld, this would seem to be a very equivocal argument in favor of virtue. It is true we may not be fully able to understand why there should be a necessity of uniformity in law, so that it may not distinguish in favor of good enterprises against bad ones. But it seems very much more difficult to understand why a power of overruling such uniformity, if it really exist and be exercised at all in favor of good enterprises, should ever fail to be exercised. In other words, the excuse from necessity at once ceases when we find it is not always a necessity; and so color is given to the inference that the claims of virtue and vice are equal, if an interposition which no necessity prevents, and which is sometimes used, be not always used in favor of virtue.

I am not ignorant that the foregoing exhibition is in contradiction with views to which not a few cling with great tenacity. But were this the place, and were my object at all polemical, they might be fortified by a variety of considerations. I content myself at present with this single additional suggestion. If supernatural interposition be rightly claimed in behalf of certain enterprises on the ground of their meritoriousness, so that, the true Equivalents being withheld, they may still be helped to success by such adventitious aid, why is there not the same reason for a similar interposition in behalf of individuals? Why are we not justified in expecting that a man who has failed to pay that price which Nature has appointed as the one sole price for certain rewards, as, for instance, personal effort, that is, who has withheld the true Equivalent, and so is disappointed of the return, — why are we not justified in expecting that this man shall be endowed with what he has thus forfeited, by the exertion of supernatural power, and so shall have patience, or reverence, or self-respect bestowed upon him from without? We certainly never do expect this. We are content in these instances to accept law in all its rigor, and both our pity and our disgust are excited towards the man who, leading a life of inglorious ease, whines because he lacks the firm muscle and robust health of his more active neighbor; or who, having never practised self-denial of any sort, covets the sweets that fall to his lot who has not been guilty of such neglect. And yet this man, thus a sufferer, is not always without excuse. Inadvertence, not viciousness, the ignorance that characterizes early years, perhaps lack of opportunity which it was the business of others to furnish, — some one of these may be chargeable with this default. And I ask again, if intervention be ever admissible, why do we not at least sometimes hope for it in such cases? If it be of such frequent occurrence as we are invited to believe it is elsewhere, why not sometimes found here? Why is it that the bare possibility of such a thing is never so much as dreamed of? Simply because, as above remarked, we here accept law, and perhaps one reason why we accept it is, that we are here not under that temptation to reject it which attends us when we become enamored of a system, or surrender our freedom by giving place to some cherished dogma.

CHAPTER V.

ROMANCE AS ILLUSTRATED IN LEGISLATION.

ROMANTIC expectations of great results in morals from mere legislative enactments could not well find more forcible exemplification than they are now finding in the class of prohibitory laws on the subject of intemperance. This class of statutes is founded upon and includes several fallacies, most of which are greatly assisted by, if indeed they do not owe their whole existence to, this romantic temper. But the identical fallacy upon which such enactments chiefly rest is this,—that society is under equal temptation to punish what may be termed vices which chiefly affect the subjects of them, as to punish crimes which directly affect and injure society itself. The temptation to use alcoholic stimulants is quite as strong in the individual as is the temptation to commit crime. But there are a vastly larger number who are subject to the first-named temptation than to the other and last named. And the motive which impels society to punish the criminal is very much stronger, and very much less capricious, than the motive which animates it to restrain the drunkard. The temptation, then, which must be overcome by law is much larger in the aggregate in one case than it is in the other, while the motive resting upon society is very much less in one case than it is in the other. In proportion as there are more drunkards to be restrained than there are criminals to be punished, in the same proportion the law ought to be more on the alert in the case first named than in the last; whereas precisely the reverse of this is true, and in the very nature of the case must always continue to be true. Intemperance doubtless affects injuriously both life and property. It makes both of them less secure. But it does this in a very different way from that in which theft, and murder, and arson, and forgery do it. It is a revolting sight to see a drunkard in his beastliness. But it is much more than revolting for a man to look upon his house in ruins by the torch of the incendiary. It stirs our indignation when we are made to behold a man squandering upon his appetite for rum what ought to have been used in the support of his family. But we are much more than indignant when, by the skill of the forger, or the hardihood of the midnight burglar, we are made to lose our property.

And yet, with so much greater incentive to punish and restrain crime, greater in that crime touches us so much more sensitively, we often fail to inflict the penalty. The motive to punish, even in these cases, does not always come up in its stringency to the motive which animates the offender. Under some plea of mercy, — some intervention of sympathy, which is always glad to seize hold of palliating circumstance or technical error, even this criminal, whom society is so much interested in having punished, often escapes. Thus it seems that laws and penalties against crimes, even with the stronger motive to strengthen them, are not equal to what is demanded of them; and much less will they avail against mere vices.

And surveyed by the clear-seeing eye of pure reason, this objection would in itself suffice to bring instant and complete rejection to this class of statutes. Men who are quite familiar with the difficulty of uniformly enforcing laws against crimes would see at once how the difficulty must be greatly increased in relation to mere vices, only that sentiment comes in to obscure the mental vision. And at this point it is that political agitators, bent upon their own personal aggrandizement, make their appeal to the emotions; and by timely aid from the romantic element, strive to extricate themselves from the logical dilemma which they are by no means ignorant of, but which they sedulously keep out of sight. They never pretend even to meet this point. The staple of their argument is, harrowing details of the evils which the great curse inflicts upon humanity, and these, constantly reiterated, hold the emotions up to furnace-heat. Under the excitement thus produced by the rant of the platform, men are easily wrought up to believe, what they for the time doubtless both honestly and earnestly desire. The evil is immense. An easy and an absolute cure is promised; the only labor, the only sacrifice required at their hands, being that they shall at the appointed day deposit a certain ballot for certain individuals who are in favor of certain measures. This is all they have to do.

And although they have been doing it steadily for thirty years or more, and nothing has been gained except by the agitators, they — that is to say, the masses who are thus duped by their crafty leaders — are sanguine as ever; and this of course. There is no reason to expect a surrender of their notions on the subject during, or at the end of, the next thirty years, unless they should at last conclude to cut loose from romance and listen a moment to logic. How long a time the distemper may be expected to run, it is impossible to predict. Of one thing we may be certain: it will not come to an end when new and better arguments are brought to bear upon it, but only when, by a general elevation of intelligence in the community, a more correct perception is reached of the demands of the question, and of the nature of the truths which appertain to it. We hardly think it worth while to argue with a man to disprove the possibility of discovering perpetual motion. The demonstration rests upon mathematical certainty, but its force does not reach his mind who is ignorant of, or refuses to accept, the premises upon which it rests. We say at once, in such a case, Let the man first acquire a knowledge of the laws of matter, and the rest will follow; but until then all argument is wasted breath. It is precisely the same in a question of political ethics.

The belief in witches and witchcraft, which for more than fifteen hundred years held firm possession of the minds of men, and was supposed to rest upon Bible authority, and the manner and causes of its final disappearance, illustrate what I am here saying. No new argument directed against it was the signal for its overthrow. So far as reasoning could go, that had long since been exhausted, and it was only when by a higher illumination, and a generally increased power of perception, men were brought to the point of understanding and appreciating what had been previously written, that they abandoned their former belief. They were under as strong a motive to escape from the accursed thing as could possibly be presented, and to our eyes it seems hardly less than incredible that the imagination should have so long held such tyrannical sway over reason. But a belief in the miraculous which then held captive the minds of even educated men, and a general taint of superstition, supplanted the reasoning faculties; and while this condition of things lasted, there was no power anywhere to contend against the frightful heresy under which thousands and tens of thousands of innocent persons were subjected to the death penalty under every conceivable form of aggravated torture. The historic details which belong to the annals of those times are absolutely too terrible to contemplate. Luther, and Baxter, and John Wesley, among theologians, and such men as Sir Matthew Hale among the laity, were firm believers in the heresy; Wesley having once remarked, "They well know, whether Christians know it or not, that the giving up of witchcraft is in effect giving up the Bible." So Luther himself once exclaimed, "I would have no compassion on these witches; I would hang them all," — an eccentricity of belief we might be surprised at in so learned a man, only that we are somewhat prepared for it by the well-known anecdote related of him, that, being once molested by the presence of the Devil, he hurled his inkstand at the arch-enemy; the stain upon the wall in the castle of Wartburg still remaining to attest the truth of the story.

The illustration I have here introduced might be greatly extended, — the history of witchcraft furnishing most pregnant and at the same time melancholy proof of the fallacies and grotesque absurdities, not to speak of crimes, into which men may be led by taking romance and sentimental aspirations for their guide, instead of following the light of reason and the dictates of common sense. And as this heresy, having held sway over the human mind for the long period above mentioned, at last disappeared before the dawn of a brighter intelligence, so may we console ourselves with the thought, that more recent and scarcely less hurtful and glaring errors into which men are now betrayed by a similar romantic spirit, will, when the time is ripe, find their antidote. As remarked already, that class of statutes termed "prohibitory laws" for the suppression of intemperance, are indebted for their existence to-day almost entirely to this spirit, — to an unreasoning determination to wrest penal laws to an illegitimate purpose, to a purpose for which they are all unsuited. "The instrument which these would-be reformers, these self-styled and self-glorifying philanthropists, have most often sought to make available for their purpose, is that of legislation, or, in some shape or other, political enginery. Under the 'droppings' of some august council-chamber or legislative hall, the sanitary herb is looked for whose potent spell is to relieve mankind forever of the curse under which they have hitherto rested. With the most overwhelming proofs all about us that a heaven-descended law, — a law devised in the far remote counsels of eternity; a law in perfecting which was exhausted the fulness of a divine wisdom and an infinite knowledge; a law suited to the thing created by Him who was the Creator; a law exemplified, illustrated, and enforced, in a manner no other law has ever been, by the life and death of the great Lawgiver himself; a law, too, so simple that he who runs may read,— with the most overwhelming proofs all about us that such a law, in the course of eighteen hundred years, instead of curing, has only partially alleviated these evils, we still go about in the hope to find the yet unrevealed secret lurking somewhere in the dark, labyrinthine passages of some petty statute of human invention. Putting their trust in these earth-born enactments, panoplied in parchment, and bulwarked about with huge tomes of man's wisdom, we have seen the mightiest nations go down successively into the dust; and in proof that their fate shall never become ours, we confidently point to another parchment, to other tomes, and to other similar enactments." [1]

Now it is evident that all this attempt to legislate the world into morality is in sheer violation of the law of equivalents, nor should we hear of such attempts were this law once universally understood and accepted. For it is plain to every one, that this is only a species of force, thinly disguised perhaps, in nowise to be distinguished from force as it was in former times sought to be pressed into the service of religion by hot-headed zealots

[1] I do not know that any apology is needed for thus transcribing from "Maine Law in the Balance," written by myself many years ago, the above extract. It would, however, be an omission without excuse, should I fail to acknowledge my obligation to Mr. Lecky, whose very interesting and instructive volumes on "Rationalism in Europe" have furnished some of the facts as well as hints for this chapter.

and merciless fanatics; and how they were guilty of violating this law has been already remarked upon. Besides, men do sometimes recognize the law. Upon some new invention being offered in physical science, the first test it must comply with is this: Will it work? Is it adapted to do what it professes? And in like manner we should propound these questions in moral science, were there no sentiment, no romance, to impart obliquity to the vision. Then, instead of appeals to passion and to prejudice, — instead of galvanizing men into unnatural fervor, and constantly adding fagots to the flame to raise their zeal to a higher point,—we should seek to make them acquainted with the logical necessities of the case, and our appeals would be made to reason and common sense.

CHAPTER VI.

POLITICAL OR GOVERNMENTAL EQUIVALENTS.

It is not an uncommon error to suppose that there are very many Equivalents of value to the individual which are of no value to the state. The qualities of the citizen, possibly his virtues, may be deemed worthy of notice when a selection is to be made for responsible positions; but for those who are left behind, who are not sent to the national Congress, or made into presidents or governors, — they surely have nothing to do with the stability or prosperity of the government. What the state needs, and what it lives and grows by, — so runs the prescription, — is great statesmen, skilful pilots, sagacious contrivers, wise counsellors, learned judges, shrewd diplomatists. Vast learning, the accumulation of centuries laid carefully away in fire-proof vaults, valuable archives duly ranged and labelled on dusty shelves, treaties with foreign powers, constitutional guaranties, and varied enactments as to what may be done and what may not, — this, and much more like this, is the pabulum upon which states feed, and in feeding prosper. These, yes, these — most astonishing hallucination !— are the identical means, using which the state shall not collapse and pass away into dust and ashes. These are not mere scaffolding,— mere external props and mechanical aids,—but they are the bone, and the muscle, and the marrow, the tough physical integuments, yea, the real, veritable soul of the thing. In a word, these are the downright Equivalents for growth, for grandeur unknown before, for prosperity unlimited, for an enduring perpetuity. A Webster, a Clay, a Calhoun, the whole succession of illustrious leaders, pass away into the embrace of death, and shocked by the gap thus occasioned, we tremblingly ask how shall it be filled, or inquire with solicitude whether the old ship will safely ride at her moorings till others come to fill their place.

Do I mean here and now to question the value of the service such as these men render? Never! Do I mean that the outward forms of organic law and constitutional provisions are useless? Again I say, Never! But I deny that they are, in any just sense, Equivalents for that we are confidently counting upon. And so, when it suits us, we all deny it, if not in words, by a logical conclusion. For what can all these forms, nay, what can the almost divinely inspired intellects of such men as I have just named, give us more or better than truth? What more or better than truth do we ask from them? But what is truth worth, unless it is obeyed? Nay, what is it worth if obeyed, and how shall it become for us anything but a cause of stumbling, a spear to transfix us on its glittering point, unless we qualify it and interpret it by its connection with, and dependence upon, other truths? And besides, is there not already on every side vast store of truth lying waste which no man uses or thinks of using, — an absolutely unproductive, dead capital, paying no interest year in and year out? Here precisely we find greater accumulation of dead capital than anywhere else, and yet hope to better our condition by adding to it, and not by utilizing it, just as though truth, so that there were only enough of it, should become conviction! But if truth itself is thus in some sort a doubtful equivalent, is infected with a certain impotency when brought into the circle of man's finity, then how shall the bearers and exhibitors of truth, and all argument also in its favor, hope to escape the same infection?

"Patience, humility, a reverential spirit, self-denial, self-control — all these to be sure are very well in their place. They are especially becoming in the Church, and are perhaps ornamental and entitled to credit elsewhere, but as contributions to the commonwealth they count as nothing." Thus we carelessly form our estimates. Thus we oracularly announce our decisions. Thus we insolently and audaciously undertake to divide between what is serviceable and what is worthless; the measure of both, in our minds, being chiefly determined by the grandeur and external pomp which severally belong to each. Were the Law of Equivalents fully understood, how would such estimates be confounded, and brought into derision! We should then be made to see that, in yonder chamber of sickness, a helpless sufferer from painful, protracted disease is offering a richer contribution, even to the state, than many an expensive, windy demagogue, aye, than many an eloquent favorite of the day, either on the platform or in the pulpit, can ever aspire to. For we must come back to this at last: it is what is real that counts. It is what is real that affects men's lives, and the life of states or communities. With so much all about us that seems to contradict the assertion, it is still true that even the impressible multitude, whose admiration is bestowed upon every glittering pageant, yields its homage at last to that only which is real. But it is homage, not admiration, that lasts till to-morrow, and yields the imperishable product. No man ever lived, or ever will live, who was brought into the presence of reality, and went away as empty as he came. It is impossible. But passive endurance, patience under disappointment and long-deferred hope, a reverent spirit bowing before acknowledged majesty that is its superior, the honest contrition of an erring and penitent heart making voluntary retribution for its offence, — these and kindred exhibitions of a lofty moral development have belonging to them this element of reality against which no man is proof. However the affectation of them provokes ridicule and disgust, the man who demonstrates his lawful claim to their possession brings an element of strength to society which the more noisy demonstration of conceited, vaporing demagogue may despair of imitating. The most carefully prepared sermon that ever fell from the lips of learned and eloquent preacher, let his sincerity be fairly questioned, let it appear that his effort is for hire, and in the performance of a mere professional engagement, and, except for the wages it brings to the speaker, it might almost as well have remained in the author's brain from whence it sprung. What is real, — that it is which counts, that it is which turns multitudinous wheels and innumerable spindles, and by keeping alive man's heart, keeps industry alive, everywhere; but all else is water running to waste, and emptying itself into the broad sea out of man's sight and thoughts forever.

"At last" — such is the thinly disguised belief — "at last the world is about to emerge from the darkness in which it has been so long groping. The chains with which it has been hitherto bound are to be snapped asunder. True indeed it is, the lives of such men as Aristotle, and Plato, and Seneca, and Socrates, demonstrate a wisdom belonging to the past, but theirs was not the wisdom of modern times. There has been an advance made, and all the acquisitions of the past are imputed and transmitted to us, — are carried over to our credit, and realized for our benefit. Civilization to-day is not a something indebted for its life and power of usefulness to what it feeds upon to-day; but it is rather a force of itself, by some unexplained process having its springs within itself, — a trained servant to do certain work for us, — a movement quite apart from the lives of men; or, if not this, it has acquired a momentum from the combined influence of all past ages, which cannot be lost again, but will go on without any help from us."

And it seems on the whole quite necessary to attach to it some such significance, else it were difficult to maintain the assumption already alluded to, of a more certain and more rapid advance for the world than it has yet reached. The two ideas are very closely connected, — that the world is getting on very fast, and that it is doing so by some help extraneous to itself. Thus it has become a favorite saying, that "we are standing on other men's shoulders," a form of expression which seems to be used by many as signifying a process of intellectual addition, and in a sense quite beyond what is justifiable. A modern philosopher is himself, plus Plato, plus Aristotle. The calculation is arithmetical, and statistics in the moral world have a numerical basis, just as they have in the material. As two men of the required stature were worth twice one to Frederick of

Prussia, who demanded that a certain regiment should be composed of soldiers six feet high, so the wisdom and experience of the past affords an assured stock in trade for modern capitalists and speculators in moral science to begin with; what they have in hand of their own being so much surplus.

But under the Law of Equivalents there is no such provision. There is no possibility of standing upon other men's shoulders in any such sense as that supposed, nor indeed in any other sense, with hope of any but the smallest results. If this were true in any but a very inferior sense, there would seem to be no reason why the onward march of civilization should not be steady and uniform, instead of being always marked as it has been by constant fluctuations. The lessons to be derived from the history of past ages have doubtless a value belonging to them. But as no man can buy for any price however extravagant another man's experience, or even borrow it for a single moment, so no more can a nation appropriate to its use the experience of another nation. The word itself, in the very significance of it, denies any such possibility. Nor is there any known place of deposit for the accumulated wisdom of the past, any appointed reservoir for the reception and preservation of aggregated moral truths, resorting to which we may, in a certain mechanical way, appropriate to our own use the labors of another. I say, in a certain mechanical way, by which is meant they must be assimilated and converted into our own substance by a process of mental digestion, which renders necessary an experimental operation of our own. They do not pass by transfer; they are not the subjects of conveyance.

It has already been explained, that the views we are attempting to present are directed chiefly against a romantic element in the American character, — an element which we suppose belongs to it in an eminent degree, and whose unwonted development we have attributed in great measure to the effect of contagion. Familiarity with the vast and the stupendous everywhere about us, both in the enterprises themselves which engage men's attention, in the extent of the field where they are displayed, and in the mighty agents offering themselves for our employment, — all these arouse and excite the mind almost to bewilderment. Not stopping to reflect how very slight is the analogy between the spiritual and the material world, and how certain habits of thought to which we have become used in the latter are utterly inapplicable to the former, we still insist upon wrenching these habits, and the laws which belong to them, to our purpose. Indeed, a Scotch writer of some note, without aid from American romance, tells us in set phrase that, in the progress we have thus far witnessed in the material world, we find the evidence of a similar coming progress in the spiritual world.

And this element of romance we allude to, this habit of ignoring logic and giving free rein to sentiment, of making the hope father to the thought, never crops out more saliently than when, forming our estimate of the value of republican institutions, we set down to their credit the civilization, and all the fruits of it, we are enjoying to-day. Shutting our eyes to the great fact that synchronously with the American experiment, in its purely political aspect, were developed other forces of almost terrific energy, we find a sweet gratification both for our vanity and for an indolent spirit which shirks the labor of investigation, by pointing always and exclusively to the mere political birth as the source of all these gifts — all this wealth.

The subject we are considering is worth a moment's attention in this connection, for it will be seen that very many, and not one only, have been the equivalents paid by us for the great whole now finally reduced to our possession. Let us, then, contemplate the auspices under which the experiment was inaugurated; let us attempt a somewhat rapid grouping of these various forces, and so be conducted to a more discriminating, perhaps more correct and wholesome, estimate than the former and more careless one. It was then, in the first place, at a period when the world had just emerged from a philosophy which amused itself with, and wasted itself upon, the most refined subtleties and barren discussions about essences and entities, and had fairly entered upon that new track upon whose guide-boards were inscribed, in letters of living light, — Fruit, Progress. Almost simultaneously with the new system thus introduced by Bacon, appeared upon the stage its innumerable handmaids, by whose aid it was at once illustrated and established, and pushed rapidly forward to the most signal triumph that has ever attended any mere human invention.

And of these, first in order of time, as it was undoubtedly first in importance, was the discovery and settlement of an entire continent, the infinite variety of whose resources was equalled only by their incalculable extent. A mere hunting-ground for the red man, whose noiseless arrow and soft-treading moccasin, leaving no trace behind, so well symbolized his life, it had hitherto found no place, either upon the map of the geographer or in the calculations of the statist and political economist. But now the scene was to change apace. A mightier than the red man was at hand, who came to rouse with no gentle summons the slumbering giant, and to unlock those priceless treasures which through a long night of untold ages had lain concealed in his vast storehouses. And as men listened to the accounts of the New World, — as story after story, each not only confirming, but adding to the one that had preceded it, proclaimed the wondrous birth, — as they heard of its immense area, equalled only by the grandeur and sublimity of its scenery; of its majestic rivers, rivalled only by its extensive seacoast; of its fertile soil, its healthful and diversified climate; of its far-sweeping forests, its broad lakes, and its mountains to their imaginations stored with gold, — they were filled with amazement not less than had the cause of it been but just upheaved from the depths of ocean. Not a new island merely, where the sea-gull might deposit her eggs, or the fisherman dry his nets, but an entire continent, equal to one half the then known land upon our globe, had suddenly emerged from a watery waste to their view, — a fact whose importance we may suppose, indeed, was at once felt by the mere compiler of charts, the mere physical geographer. But was this all, or rather, though not revealed to their eyes, was it not a fact, too, whose bearings upon man's social and political condition were calculated to prove still more important? Undoubtedly it was; and altogether apart from the question as to what form of government might be set up, a new element had been brought to light, henceforth to be thrown into the crucible of civilization, which could with no more propriety be overlooked by the civilian than these bold headlands, these island-dotted bays, these pebbled beaches, these commodious harbors, could be overlooked by the maker of charts for the mariner, or of maps and globes for the schoolboy; and these far-sweeping forests, these deep-flowing, wide-mouthed rivers, these immense lakes, and the thundering voice they continually utter, were not apt symbols only, but the prophetic proof also, of that new tide of energy and enterprise which, having its birth under the keel of the Genoese navigator, was destined, like the ocean he had come to explore, to encompass the whole earth with its arms, to send its swelling wave far up into a thousand channels, and without fainting, to bear upon its buoyant bosom the heaviest burdens.

Upon the same stage, too, and bringing a most significant aid to that just mentioned, there now appeared another handmaid, and mechanism, promoted from the ash-hole where, like Cinderella, she had been long banished, — Mechanism, so jeered and flouted at by the spiritual Greek and the philosophizing Roman, now robed in imperial purple, and exercising a dominion which king or despot never swayed; Mechanism, with sinewy arm and ten thousand nimble fingers, — she, too, came to assist in the inauguration of the new epoch, until it has happened that this our immense territory, vast as is its extent, and varied as are its requirements, is spotted all over with triumphal columns commemorative of her success, and its whole surface, even every corner of it, has become one vast diagram to illustrate her glorious march. To the South, whose fat soil mourned for aid, she sent an Arkwright with his spinning-jenny and a Whitney with his cotton-gin. To the rolling prairie of the West, whose bursting granaries offer a supply for the world's wants, she sent a McCormick with his reapers; while as we approach the commercial states bordering upon the Atlantic, or contemplate the manufacturing interests of New England, we are fairly overwhelmed by the variety and the splendor of her gifts.

And where were fitting espousals to be found for so queenly a presence? That these might not be wanting, there had occurred, too, another birth, and the Steam-king stood forth to claim his lawful bride; and need it be said with what pomp and ceremony the nuptials have been celebrated, or how they have been blessed with a giant progeny, who have their abode on land and sea, on lake and river, in the valley and on the mountain top, almost throughout the habitable globe!

But without extending the enumeration further, when we consider that this is the period when the art of printing has reached its full development; and still more when we consider how all these and innumerable other kindred agencies have had their birth either simultaneously, or at such wisely adjusted intervals as, by their subsequent union and their reciprocal aid each to the other, to constitute one sublime, gigantic, and doubly effective whole,— suggesting the thought that Nature, long enslaved and condemned to grind in her prison-house, was at length rallying and concentrating all her mighty energies for one final struggle against her enemies, — I say, when we consider these things, is it not evident that the time is still distant when we may strike the balance, and determine what part Republicanism, and what part these her allies have performed, or are performing in the great drama now being enacted before our eyes?

I am perfectly aware that, in denying to the mere forms and machinery of government the dignity and true value of Equivalents, I am only stating that to which very many, possibly the majority, have been long in the habit of yielding theoretically their assent. That virtue and intelligence are the only stable foundations of a free government, that "eternal vigilance is the price of liberty," — these are maxims which are ever upon our lips, and which, speculatively, nobody ever thinks of rejecting. But even by that class who are most ready to receive these maxims, and who desire to see them brought more constantly into practical operation, it seems not unlikely that some of the remarks in this chapter may appear too strongly put. Whatever persistently makes claims for itself, even if the claim be not founded in justice, is very apt to win final assent, and all the more certainly when the arrogator is supported by a certain outside glitter, by the dazzle of artificial belongings and equipments, and by highly remunerative rewards. And besides all this, the mere external machinery of government, — diplomacy in all its stilted stateliness, treaties with foreign nations, acts of Congress, decisions of judicial tribunals, — all these, with a certain grandeur of movement belonging to them, are the visible sources from whence the state derives its support and its authority; and thus making constant appeal to the senses, it would afford small cause for surprise if even those who withhold absolute homage from these instrumentalities should yet become unduly enamored of them, and should find themselves offended by what may appear to be a too free criticism of their merits.

A not unnatural nor altogether unjustifiable national vanity contributes towards a similar result. When we challenge a comparison with other nations, it is the "system" we have adopted to which we point in maintaining such challenge. Are we, as Americans, better off than any other people? Both we and those with whom we invite a comparison have in mind as the cause of this superiority the single fact of Republicanism as against a less free system; and thus by an almost inevitable intellectual process we give to mere form a credit which belongs not to form, but to something very different. And it is hardly to be expected that even sober-minded people should always escape the operation of some one or all of these disturbing influences; and so, while they will concede in the main the justice of my remarks on this topic, would have liked them better had they been more guardedly expressed. It may possibly appear to them that, in applying the Law of Equivalents to this subject, I have been thinking only of magnifying its importance, and so have exceeded just bounds in my animadversions upon certain agencies to which I have denied the name of Equivalents. It may therefore be worth while to inquire for a moment upon what deeper grounds the whole question rests.

And unless I am laboring under a grave error, the question resolves itself into this: Is there any sense in which pure intellect can be considered in itself a foundation of government; any sense in which it can be accepted, no matter how vast the heights to which it may have attained, as a substitute for moral elements; any sense in which the absence of personal contributions by the individual can be atoned for by the wisdom of the council chamber, the sagacity of the diplomat, or the learning of the statesman?

Of all attempts, all modern attempts certainly, to make out man's intellect to be the only real foundation of progress for the race, that of the late Mr. Buckle is most marked by various learning and minute research. So much is uniformly conceded, even by those who most differ with him. And what was one of the most prominent, and at the same time most pleasing, conclusions to which his generalizations conducted this eminent scholar,

— a conclusion, too, quite justifiable, the correctness of his premises being only once established? It was nothing less than this, — that wars, upon any considerable scale, would in the future be nearly or quite unknown. And what have been the facts that have followed so closely upon the heels of this pleasing prediction? Hardly has the grass grown green upon the grave of the learned and lamented author when two of the most extensive and most destructive wars the world has ever witnessed came to offer a sad but instructive commentary upon the theory to whose support he brought so much industry and so much learning, and in whose support he was interrupted by his death. Facts had been laboriously gleaned from every quarter of the globe and every period of time; authors, ancient and modern, had been cited in such numbers as to fairly weary the reader, and to astonish him at the beholding of such minute and varied research; ingenuity had done its best in weaving these materials into a compact theory, and the result at last only demonstrates that the theory was false. Intellect, indeed, achieves its stupendous triumphs. Its brilliant march is signalized by events that excite our wonder and our admiration, — that stir our enthusiasm as it has never been stirred before. But it reaches not to the subjection of human passions. The lust of dominion, the promptings of avarice and revenge, — these and other base spirits are not yet exorcised from the hearts of men; and the crafty, audacious, unprincipled demagogue cherishes his foul aspirations as unmolested by fear of failure; as undeterred by the public scorn, as ever.

There is, then, very much that every government, and especially every free representative government, needs and must have too, for which intellect, and all the forms and appliances that intellect can contrive, is not an Equivalent. And this is all that is here affirmed.

Has intellect, and all the fruits of intellect, as exhibited in the profuseness of its gifts to man, with its boasted art of printing as an all-serviceable ally; with the restraints it has furnished through the more closely connected and the more widely extended commercial relations of which it has been the origin; with all the diversified activity of brain which has been its instrument in every department, — has it been found equal to the extermination of grovelling propensities and brutish desires; or, as Mr. Buckle presents the picture, has it quenched the flames of war, and so freed the world from the most terrible scourge that afflicts humanity? Let the desolations war but lately brought upon the sunny fields of the southern portion of our own land, and the track of blood and carnage and widespread ruin it only yesterday followed over the plains and vine-clad hills of France, answer the question. Is it not too painfully evident that the world has something yet to learn about Equivalents, or at least to practise in that regard, while such scenes are possible, and being possible, the same world is so little affected by them?

To enumerate here the various Equivalents that enter into the composition of Politics is quite beyond the author's design. But there is one of universal application, which, owing to certain peculiarities in the American system, has for us a special significance: I mean Compromise. Entitled by its intrinsic merits to hold a very conspicuous position, by force of certain accidents it has acquired an odor in our nostrils it by no means deserves. It will be understood at once that I here have in mind nothing in the past history of the American people. What good or what evil certain historical compromises may have brought to the nation, evidently affects not at all the general truth.

And this rests upon a foundation that cannot be shaken; to wit, that for man there is nothing absolute. No single truth even is absolute for a finite intelligence. It requires to be brought into the great family of truths, and to be surveyed in connection with them, that we may thus attain to its relative value, which is all that we can do. It is by a neglect of this simple but absolutely necessary precaution that fanaticism — the greatest scourge that in all past ages has afflicted humanity

— gets its birth. The claim set up is, that we may adopt and apply a measurement which is for the employment only of the Infinite mind. It acts upon the hypothesis that what is true is, in the nature of the case, incapable of being applied too rigidly or too exhaustively. Limited as are man's faculties in the acquisition of truth, and shallow as is his understanding of it, the application of it never staggers him who falls a victim to this fanatical temper. He runs his line as a surveyor runs his; all that lies on this side being wrong, all on that side right. Molluscs, invertebrate organization, — these, and others like these, are the words he is fond of. He is immovably fixed in his conclusions, and utters his verdicts with an oracular wisdom. In a lofty tone he inveighs against a cowardly, unmanly yielding to circumstances, for what is true to-day is true to-morrow, and truth is to be followed and obeyed at all times. He loves to think admiringly of his own stern inflexibility and his magnanimous adherence to the dogmas of a sect, or the decrees of a platform; the mere article of belief being by him promoted into the highest place of all. Charity is with him little less than a deadly sin, any suggestion of palliating circumstance, of sudden temptation, of human infirmity, being received by him with a heavy frown; while whatever projects beyond his own Procrustean bed he lops off with merciless severity. Such is the fanatic, — a foe to all compromise, an enemy to society, a curse to the state, a poison in the church.

But if we deprecate all this in private life, and lament the sad havoc there introduced by this merciless, undeviating rigor, we shall easily perceive how it is not less fatal in the world of politics. For there it is, if possible, still more true, that for man there is nothing absolute. The ship on the sea, — how seldom does the wind that propels her lie directly abaft; how for the most part must her progress be the result of only side winds, which finally bring her into port, only because she from time to time abandons the direct course which leads thither, and extracts the most that the case admits of out of these not all adverse, not all favorable air-currents. And besides these winds are also currents of the ocean, not less demanding the mariner's attention, if he would avoid shipwreck on this treacherous shoal or that hidden ledge. In fine, this sailor, this diplomat of the ocean, watches not heaven only, and so inquires what the weather portends; but he is careful also to cast an eye around him and beneath him. The statesman, the political pilot, is always under a similar necessity. He, no more than that other mariner, gets all his inspiration or all his maxims from heaven above, but he remembers that to-day, at least, there is very much, quite far removed from and disconnected with heaven, that he must take note of. He understands that the absolute has not been reached; that to choose skilfully, to select wisely, is his first duty: his highest wisdom is to know what to accept. By indirection, not necessarily in the worst sense of that term, but by surrendering a little here, with a view to greater ultimate profit — by trimming his sails to catch the half-favorable breeze, he gains what headway is possible.

And this is always so. It is true of all governments, and indeed of whatever man puts his hand to. But the truth gets to itself special emphasis in its application to the American system. Under a system of confederated communities like our own, there is, over and above that necessity which is found everywhere, a new demand for a spirit, and a practice too, of compromise. We claim and calculate upon receiving the diversified gifts which such a confederated union of forces has the power of bestowing. We reap and gather into our lap, not only material products from material fields in wonderful variety and abundance, but we get to ourselves also, what is certainly not less valuable, diversity of intellect, and opposite types of sentiment and emotion, as these are severally begotten and ripened under tropical suns and polar snows, under Eastern maturity and a younger and fresher birth in the far West; and it is but reasonable that thus receiving these great Equivalents, — for such they well deserve to be called, — we should pay the price which alone can perpetuate them.

And whether it is reasonable or not, the condition is one we cannot escape from, if we would retain the advantages. The not only eloquent but deeply significant words of the departed statesman must become for us more than ever household words, and we must "know no North, no South, no East, no West," if we are not prepared to surrender the fruits which this great agglomeration of forces is capable of bestowing. The price — the inexorable price, admitting of no substitution whatever — is compromise; a surrender of lesser interests, a partial sacrifice of local claims, for the sake of the wider and more general benefit. We must bring the Equivalent in one hand, if with the other we would receive the reward.

But there is nothing compulsory upon us in this regard. Nature will not compel us to accept the offered boon, and if we choose to become the dupes of self-seeking demagogues, — to listen to mischief-making go-betweens, to minister to the claims of opposing and selfish rivalries, and so lend ourselves to the promotion of sectional interest or sectional views, — we shall but repeat that bitter experience so often illustrated which gets to itself what consolation it can under its heavy disappointment by exclaiming, "It would never have so sinned, had it known how great was the penalty of transgression."

"But," says the objector, "is principle, then, to go to the wall?" A truer form of the question would be, Does principle go to the wall? We may abandon organized government altogether, because its administration is not always and momently compatible with a strict observance of certain absolutely pure and lofty maxims; but if we decide to retain it, we must do so on the only terms that are possible. We accept society and civilization for the sake of the advantages they give us over the savage state, and we do this with full knowledge that we thereby introduce certain hurtful vices, and a long catalogue of bodily diseases, which would otherwise have never been known. We accept innumerable other things on the same conditions. Indeed we never accept anything without at the same time accepting a source of weakness and of sinning. I say again, for man there is nothing absolute. The eremite, who chooses the seclusion of his cell, and so separates himself from the world by the thickness of its walls, does not separate himself from this law of humanity; for wherever man goes, this law follows him, cleaving to him more closely than did the Old Man of the Sea to the back of Sinbad the sailor.

And is there anything in all this that implies a truancy to principle, — an abandonment of the cause and the interests of virtue? It would seem a distorted judgment, an oblique vision, an unhealthy sensitiveness of conscience, that should so affirm. Nor would such verdict seem to harmonize with acknowledgments we constantly make in the practical ordering of every-day life. We initiate enterprises, without any compunctions whatever, whose success involves not only evil consequences, but absolute criminality, which would otherwise never have happened. It is absolutely certain that in a commercial community, for instance, the revenue laws will sometimes be violated by the evasion of duties; but no man hesitates to build a ship because it may possibly become an instrument for such violation. Under the system of slavery formerly existing in these United States, there were vast numbers who held that it was sinful, — that it was the "sum and essence of all villanies;" but at the same time they were holding this opinion, they daily and hourly, and without stint, partook of the products of slave labor, luxuries as well as the necessaries of life, and thus indirectly contributed to the support of the system. But did such persons ever censure themselves for so doing, or did it once occur to them that they were thus guilty of any breach of propriety or consistency? And to-day, Mormonism practically violates principles that are held to be of sacred authority by a vast majority of the American people. But it is tolerated, and for a reason which is accepted as a sufficient reason, — that certain political maxims, certain considerations of mere worldly policy, forbid, just now at any rate, its extirpation. There is a species of economy which is described as "penny wise, pound foolish." A similar disproportion is often exhibited in the demand which is made for belief, mere speculative opinion, and for the fruits which such belief ought to yield. The world has not yet done pardoning very much to the man who believes right, be his conduct what it may.

A distinguished modern writer, while discussing a kindred topic, says: "The time will doubtless come when the man who lays the foundation-stone of a manufacture will be able to predict with assurance in what proportion the drunkenness and the unchastity of his city will be increased by his enterprise. But he will still pursue that enterprise, and mankind will itself pronounce it to be good." And in another connection the same writer observes: "That vice has often proved an emancipator of the mind, is one of the most humiliating, but at the same time one of the most unquestionable, facts in history. It is the special evil of intolerance, that it entwines itself around the holiest parts of our nature, and becomes at last so blended with the sense of duty, that, as has been finely said, 'Conscience, which restrains every other vice, becomes the prompter here.' Two or three times in the history of mankind, its destruction has involved a complete dissolution of the moral principles by which society coheres, and the cradle of religious liberty has been rocked by the worst passions of humanity."

There is a possibility that certain unguarded expressions have escaped in the chapter now brought to a close, which might imply a denial of any virtue belonging to one form of government over another. That construction would do great injustice to my meaning. A form of government does signify, but it does so because it is in accord with the sentiments and habits of thought which belong to its subjects, and not by virtue of the power it has of bestowing such sentiments and habits of thought. The saying of Sir George Cornwall Lewis, one of England's most practical statesmen until removed by his untimely death, would seem to contain all the truth that the question embraces. He said there was no such thing as a best form of government, any more than there is such a thing as a best knife. Everything depends upon the use either the government or the knife is to be put to. It is doubtless better to live under a free and elastic and accommodating system like our own, if there be virtue and enlightenment enough belonging to the people to sustain the system; but if on the contrary the system be depended upon to atone for deficiency in these respects, and so to support the people, instead of being supported by them, we should be only cheating ourselves with a gross delusion.

That the constantly reiterated panegyric of our own system, which we listen to from boyhood up, and which the great majority never have an opportunity of contrasting with other systems, should not only beget a vainglorious spirit which facts by no means always justify, but should go further than this and create a belief that a form of government possesses a virtue and a vitality intrinsically far beyond what is true, seems not unlikely to happen. The feeling insensibly but almost inevitably comes to occupy our hearts, that the government goes on in a certain mechanical way, to do a certain work for us and not by us. But the Law of Equivalents denies any such possibility. The province of this law is to discriminate, and while it does this in giving preference to one system over another, where the conditions have been complied with, it also with equal care discriminates in determining what a form of government can do, and what it cannot do.

CHAPTER VII.

ANTITHETICAL EQUIVALENTS.

The subject we are considering brings into very prominent notice the all-important principle, that for man there is nothing absolute. Seeing that this is true, and seeing that there is a large class of objects for which payment in kind is exacted, it follows that there are what may be termed Antithetical Equivalents; that is, Equivalents of such an opposite character that the holding of one, in the very necessity of the case, forbids the holding of the other. We must make a choice. We must accept loss in one direction in order to make gain in another. We receive one gift, only upon terms of a partial or entire surrender of another. This is, indeed, only the statement in a different form of a truth which nobody denies, — the limitation of the human faculties; but it includes many very important practical lessons.

As a simple illustration: a man would like very well to have the miser's wealth, but the niggardliness of spirit, the self-denial, the obloquy of the world, some one or all of which have been the price paid for that wealth,— these he will by no means consent to. But the choice must be made, and the man shall have that which he brings the price for, and nothing more.

The same truth finds a more extended illustration in personal character, where some traits are had at the expense of others; sometimes, indeed, what is in itself a weakness, or even positive blemish, being a source of strength. It has long since passed into a proverb, that impudence is better than brains, and as an instrument of success, so, indeed, it often is. How frequently, too, do we see what the phrenologists classify as a coarse organization winning full success where a more delicate, refined temperament, holding shyly aloof from the promiscuous scramble for earth's prizes, makes a failure of it, at least in the ordinary acceptation of the word! A little alloy would help some men, just as it does the gold coin. Thus, too, it is that pride and poverty go together. The proud and sensitive man finds his success in the gratification of his pride. The thrift that follows fawning is the identical thing he will not so much as touch. And so all along through the various avenues to wealth, or other sources of distinction, he finds much from which he recoils in disgust; so that, in the sense I now intend, he gets color of worthiness which his more successful rival by no means deserves.

Thus every man has his own personal identity as his own peculiar property, not to be exchanged or shuffled off for another on any terms whatever.

True, there often occurs a blending, or rather a coexistence, in the same individual, of what we pronounce incongruous traits. We speak of them as contradictory, and are in the habit of regarding them as unnatural. But not so. Feminine tenderness is often associated with masculine strength and courage, if indeed it be not true that courage never reaches its highest form except when it is thus associated. I have already made mention of Nelson, the great English commander, as an instance in point; and could all the similar instances be collected where a certain femineity of character has been found conjoined with traits more typically masculine, we should perhaps be surprised to find how largely we are indebted to this class for the most valuable gifts we ever receive; and we should thus have placed in our hands, not only a compliment to the so-called weaker sex, but an unanswerable argument in favor of retaining, at what not cost, those qualities which, originating with woman, become, when transferred over to man's use, the source of inestimable blessings.

Nor does it seem quite certain that the epicene temperament thus developed from this conjunction has received that attention from psychological writers which it deserves. During the late civil war between the Northern and Southern States, the military development was probably more rapid than ever happened before in the world's history. Many sudden reputations were won, and many hearts kindled with an ardor till then unfelt and unknown. But among them all, not one name stands out in more bold relief, and more challenges the admiration of both parties to the contest, than does that of "Stonewall" Jackson; and so, too, not one of all the thousands who mingled in that bloody strife possessed this epicene character more than he. It may be true, I suppose it is true, that there are certain departments in which this character finds special employment and shines with special lustre. But they are departments the world has always held in high esteem, and always delighted to honor. The poet, the orator, the soldier, — what a trinity is that, worshipped of men in all time past, and to be worshipped through all time to come, while Faith, and Love, and Charity, and Reverence, and Manhood survive!

But neither of these has attained the highest rank, or ever shall attain it, except only when inspired by that true, divine valor, that imperial, majestic kingliness of temper, which neither sex can claim as its own exclusive property; but which, being as it is of such wonderful excellence, is only to be had by the contributions of both. Of poets, as belonging to this class, I think should be cited, among others Dante, and Milton, and Shakespeare, and Robert Burns; of orators, Cicero, and Fox, and Burke, and Patrick Henry, and Clay, and Bossuet, and Massillon, and Whitfield; of soldiers, the two already named, Sir Phillip Sydney, Sir Walter Raleigh, and many others. The list in each of these departments might be greatly extended; and outside of them, a host of illustrious men might be named whose memory the world will not willingly let die, who owe their worthiness and their favor to this participation in woman's tenderness, and woman's enthusiasm, and woman's nobleness.

As already intimated, under this class of Antithetical Equivalents must be reckoned still others, which are had upon even severer terms, when a man may be said to owe his strength to certain weaknesses or unsoundness of character. We are constantly meeting with instances of this kind, so often, indeed, that wherever great excellence is found, we count with considerable certainty upon finding also certain flaws or blemishes, which are the inseparable concomitants, if not the actual conditions, of such excellence; just as the perfume ambergris is the product of a disease in the animal which furnishes it. Many of my readers will be reminded in this connection, of the following passage from Mr. Macaulay's "Boswell's Life of Johnson." He says: "That such a man should have written one of the best books in the world is strange enough. But this is not all. Many persons who have conducted themselves foolishly in active life, and whose conversation has indicated no superior powers of mind, have written valuable books. Goldsmith was very justly described by one of his contemporaries as an inspired idiot, and by another as a being who wrote like an angel and talked like poor Poll. La Fontaine was in society a mere simpleton. His blunders would not come in amiss among the stories of Hierocles. But these men attained literary eminence in spite of their weaknesses. Boswell attained it by reason of his weaknesses. If he had not been a great fool, he would never have been a great writer."

Now admitting that Mr. Macaulay's fondness for antithesis has imparted a taint of extravagance to his criticism, it doubtless contains much truth. And it seems a literary curiosity quite worthy of a place in the collection of Mr. D'Israeli, that Mr. Carlyle should have so patly contradicted this estimate of the English reviewer. In a notice of this same book Mr. Carlyle says: "Nay, sometimes a strange enough hypothesis has been started of him [Boswell], as if it were in virtue of these same bad qualities that he did his good work; as if it were the fact of his being among the worst men in this world that had enabled him to write one of the best books therein. Falser hypothesis, we may venture to say, never rose in human soul."

The Scotchman evidently does not believe in the Law of Equivalents. I suspect Mr. Macaulay did believe in the law.

Nothing certainly can be plainer than that a superiority in a certain direction is often made possible only by some weakness in another direction. "He never said a foolish thing, or did a wise one,"— although this was originally applied to a particular individual, the epigram would suit a vast number of others equally well. It very often happens that the best man in the world to apply to for advice is the one who in the management of his own affairs is a mere simpleton. His brains seem to be of value to everybody but himself; for when they are exercised about other people's business, his reasonings are sound, his conclusions are correct. His hints often prove to be the foundation of other men's fortunes; while his sad blunderings in all that relates to his own affairs make him the laughing-stock of men who as to brain are altogether his inferiors.

A very significant illustration of the point is found in Mr. Dickens's "Tale of Two Cities," where two characters are introduced who represent opposite poles, — Carton, the man of emotion, and of intellect too; but acting as jackal only to Stryker, the man of business, who represents the lion, and gets the lion's share. The character of Carton, finely delineated and well sustained, reveals, I think, a knowledge of human nature, and an acquaintance with the springs of human action, quite equal to anything in the whole range of fiction. The heroic self-sacrifice attributed to him the reader very readily accepts; for if any man could have given his life for a friend, it was the man who, like Carton, was in a sense conscious of his latent powers, but was conscious, too, how, under the want of any sufficient ruling passion, he had suffered his life to lapse away unsignalized by any noble achievement, — the man who, like Carton, craved with a miser's greed a worthiness that should commend him to the embrace of some single loving heart, but was hindered from attaining it by a for the most part irresistible apathy, but still an apathy which, once dispelled by a spasmodic energy, would be the means of bearing him to heights of noble action, which a more uniform and equable temperament could never reach. So out of weakness came strength; and if, in the entire range of fiction, there is anything that for beauty and pathos and heroism surpasses that last ride in the tumbril to the guillotine, when, seated by the side of the little timid sister in misfortune, he takes her hand in his, and comforts and strengthens her for the coming ordeal, I have not met with it. And I say again, a greatness and a nobleness of soul was here exhibited which no man constituted with a different temperament could ever have displayed. Carton's weakness was his strength. Thus it sometimes happens that, in seasons of commotion, when stirring events are transpiring, and unwonted occasion comes to inspire and arouse the heart, we are surprised at finding some hitherto unnoticed and almost unknown individual, rising at once into eminence, and putting to shame many who till then had seemed to be his superiors. True, we ridicule, and perhaps justly despise, the man who waits for some such great occasion; but in some instances, at least, we may suppose that, like Carton, he is contending against an apathetic temperament which nothing else is sufficient to overcome.

The suggestion which this view is calculated to convey is not without its value. In our estimate of men, they must be surveyed each one as a unit and an individual; it being impossible, by any analysis within our power, so to divide and separate between the good and the bad qualities belonging to them as to decide what might with advantage have been either omitted or added. Many very kindly and well disposed persons find much in Robert Burns, and in others similarly constituted, to invite their criticism, perhaps their censure. But he must have been a bold and venturesome experimenter who would have undertaken to meddle with that various organization which went to the making up of Scotland's favorite poet. The English people had just ground of complaint against Lord Clive and Warren Hastings; but had there been no such ground of complaint, their Indian possessions would probably show very differently upon the map of the world to-day.

And so the catalogue might be indefinitely increased of men whose lives have been specially marked by irregularities; men unsparingly condemned by society, which still is willing to accept the manifold blessings which flow to it from this source, but does not always consider how the very disease it so stigmatizes has been the price by which those benefits have been realized. The most censorious, unmerciful judge is the man who, never moved by a lofty impulse, never tempted by a consuming passion, never elevated above the dust of a tame, sordid selfishness, first thanks Heaven, instead of his own ignoble nature, that saved him from a fall; and then proceeds, with inquisitorial rigor, to sit in judgment upon what he is alike incapable of understanding or enjoying.

Again. As this Law of Equivalents is often found making very subtle and refined distinctions in the opposite mental and emotional traits which are begotten of different occupations, so that subdivision of the subject I am now considering, under the title of Antithetical Equivalents, finds also its illustration from the same source; a man by long service in one profession, or in one branch of industry, acquiring unwonted skill, and fitness, and facility in these branches, only upon terms of surrendering these qualities elsewhere. Some of the more general and universal types thus produced are too palpable to escape the most careless observation; and a sudden transfer from one occupation to another discovers to us what in familiar phrase we term a bull in a china shop. We are always prepared to find the man of action distinguished widely from the man of contemplative habits, and we severally approach one or the other as we have occasion for this or that service.

But there are nicer distinctions than these, which, pursued into their details, might yield pleasant fruit. I can at present only attempt what may prove a suggestive outline. The man who, perched upon his long-legged stool, prepares the wire, or adjusts the head, or sharpens the point of a pin, is scarcely elevated above the machinery he employs; indeed, may almost be regarded as a part of it. His movements are quite as automatic as are those of the revolving shafts and buzzing wheels around him. No demand is made upon his intellect. There is nothing to stimulate thought, to awaken emotion, or to appeal to the superstitious element in his nature. A properly contrived mechanism might perform all that he performs.

Now, bringing this man into comparison with another who is still only a subordinate operative, for instance, the sailor, we find, it is true, the same mechanical routine of duty to a considerable extent. But after all, the duties are very different in kind, and the scenes in which these two move are quite unlike. The educational results differ as widely as the two horizons do, which bound the ocean and the workshop. The experiences of the sailor are, for no two successive days even, exactly the same. The rattling of the cordage has a music in it that does not belong to steam-propelled wheels. Monotonous as is the sea, and the sky that rests upon the sea, it is a monotony very different from that of the smoke-begrimed prison-house of the artisan. Contrivance, too, and adaptation to changing circumstances, make demands more or less upon the intellect. But the difference in result is chiefly seen in the effect produced upon the emotions. The imagination of the sailor, all uncultivated as it is, is not unimpressed by the display of power he is made to be the witness of. He bows before the majesty of the storm; he listens, half in delight and half in awe, to the mysterious winds; as he paces the deck on his solitary round at night, he watches the constellations over his head, and wonders perhaps which of all those countless stars is the star of his destiñy; he is brought more than most men, and oftener than most men, face to face with danger. He is thus proverbially superstitious; he is eminently fond of the miraculous. He will not cast loose from his moorings or trip his anchor of a Friday, if he can help it; no yarns of the forecastle can in number exceed the boundlessness of his appetite, or in marvellousness surpass the capacity of his belief.

And brought into comparison with either of these men, the tiller of the soil contrasts strongly with both of them. No class is made to feel more instantly the effects of a mistake in judgment, or of tardy execution, than the agriculturist. His experiments are tested the very season that he tries them; and if they fail, the effects of such failure are not only felt at once, but are incapable of being alleviated by the various expedients which are always at hand for the man engaged in commercial pursuits — bills of accommodation, and all that, which are so familiar in city life. He is accordingly proverbial for his caution, and his sceptical, unimpressible nature; his aversion to new theories, indeed to mere theoretical knowledge at all, being often cited against him in proof of his stolidity, while he is considered a fair mark for any and everybody's ridicule for his stubborn adherence to antiquated notions. But if in all cases the punishment followed the offence as closely as it does here, certain enthusiastic speculations would receive a quite useful check; and, too, if the consequences of error were visited solely upon the heads of the authors of it, as is true in case of the farmer, the same unimpressible, conservative habits which he exhibits would find imitators elsewhere, and not without advantage. What is set down by pert lecturers and flippant advisers to sluggishness of intellect, is more correctly to be charged to close observation, quickened and sharpened by the necessities of his position. But to proceed. The three classes I have thus presented in the picture are alike composed of men toughened and matured by honest toil, but they differ each one from the other, as much as the ruddy-faced English drover, who sits there on yonder bench, quaffing his ale from his huge pewter flagon, differs from that Mississippi boatman, who for the nonce has thrown his lathy, supple form along the settee in yon whiskey drinking-saloon, the two Equivalents here at work being the climate and the beverage.

And here, as always, the Equivalent being paid, the reward is at hand; the farmer, instead of being, as he is for the most part reckoned, a mere producer of certain fruits of the earth, and so to be excused from longer attendance whenever a machine shall be devised for that purpose to take his place, furnishing to society a conservative element which we should look for in vain among the commercial classes, which last named represent the centrifugal rather than the centripetal force in the social organism. Each offers his own contribution and fills his own place; and, too, he does this by being in a sense incapacitated from filling a different or an opposite place. And it is in place to add here, that an argument is thus furnished why society should seek to make itself many-sided,— that is, should encourage a variety of pursuits, not merely for the sake of the material products they yield, but for their conservative influence also; even crime and vicious indulgences offering valuable contribution in this regard.

Similar illustrations to the above abound on every side. The sculptor, who with trained hand guides the dainty chisel, and the smith at the forge, whose brawny arm swings aloft the huge hammer, will differ in their spiritual hardly less than in their bodily development. And in this connection, we are almost inevitably reminded of Longfellow's fine lines, "The Village Blacksmith," and that other most truthful and dramatic picture by Tennyson, "The Northern Farmer."

But the distinctions I am speaking of run into much finer lines, and exist under less noticeable forms. The intellect itself furnishes these Antithetical Equivalents, and itself receives with one hand, only by surrendering with the other. Its different forms of activity yield their separate and distinct results, and illustrate, not less than the external occupations above alluded to, this law. If there were any exception to this remark, we might suppose that the lawyer, for instance, would furnish it, since not only a severity but a diversity of labor and of knowledge is required at his hands, in a degree far beyond what is exacted in any other profession, and we might therefore hastily infer that to him the doctrine would not apply. But it by no means follows that the lawyer is prepared by his professional studies and discipline to be a safe investigator of general truths, or to thoroughly conduct every intellectual process. And the same may be said of the theologian and the physician. Nor do I here allude to every particular bias the mind receives in favor of this or that dogma or system, but only to that specific training in a certain direction to which each of these professions is compelled to submit. Neither of them directs his efforts to the discovery or to the advocacy of general or universal propositions. Their inquiries are of a professional, circumscribed nature, rather than of a philosophical and catholic nature, and to a certain extent disqualify them for the examination of this last named class of subjects. I have somewhere met with the remark, that great lawyers are seldom the most successful statesmen; a fact which, if it be true, finds its explanation in what I am now saying.

And the same thought may be pursued a little further. Our attention has just been given to Equivalents which are the result of different intellectual types. But those which depend upon the emotions are quite as strongly marked. A melancholy temperament will be increased rather than diminished by devoting the attention to a class of subjects which in the nature of them refuse to be pursued to any clear, final issue, or which leave it doubtful to the mind of the inquirer whether he is making any real progress. On the contrary, the investigator of the exact sciences, the chemist for instance, who is able to report progress daily, receives a mental stimulant which acts strongly upon his emotions. An elasticity of feeling is imparted to his whole life, not only inspiring him with fresh ardor for additional explorations, but furnishing that wholesome pabulum of success for the heart to feed upon, which no man is entirely above the want of.

A broader application of the law under consideration is furnished by two opposite types of civilization. Monasticism, and the intense Industrialism of the present age, do not merely exhibit a difference in the fruits they severally yield, which an idle curiosity may amuse itself withal in estimating, but these fruits can by no possibility be enjoyed by the same people at one and the same time. A civilization cannot be at the same time new and old. As it is the sad experience of every man, that adult years can bring no such pleasure to his heart as he gathered along the paths of childhood; as he finds himself reserved, not confiding; artificial, not natural, suspicious and critical, not credulous and complaisant; living ever in the future and not in the present; he knows the price he has paid for manhood, and sometimes, at least, he feels that he has paid quite enough for it, even if he go not so far as to wish his childhood back again.

A not unlike reflection may find place at times in the mind of a man who is living under an advanced civilization. The fruits which it pours into his lap in such overflowing abundance are visibly, undeniably there; the price of them has been paid, the transaction is irrevocably sealed. Is he never tempted to ask whether, in the retrospect, the price he has paid, or which rather society has paid, does not seem " quite enough"? Does it never occur to him how a little surrender here, might be followed by much larger gain there? But it may not be. Station yourself on Broadway or on Wall Street in yonder thronged metropolis. Watch that living current which, like a swollen river, rushes madly on in its headlong course. Listen to that multitudinous roar of its waves, as they clash and gride along against the bulwarked walls of brick and stone on either side, through the long day hoarse-bellowing far afield, and mounting skyward to break the stillness of the upper air. Note these glittering equipages, these accumulated stores of merchandise; this search for pleasure, or this greed of gain, which mark the countenances of men; see on every side these evidences of physical prosperity and greatness, these signs of wealth, these tokens of material substance unsurpassed since time began. Is all this worthless, a mere good-for-nothing cheat? Is it all a sham? No, a thousand times no. But the price of it, — do we flatter ourselves that all this has come into our hands without our paying for it? Do we forget the Law of Equivalents, of Antithetical Equivalents? Or do our thoughts sometimes for a moment travel back to the monastery of the olden time, and do we call to mind its lonely inhabitant keeping his wasting, solitary vigils far into the night, taking to himself therefrom such reward as he may?

And perhaps the historical illustration here suggested may not without profit be followed a little more in detail. It is obvious and simple enough, since it is by looking at its own specific progress in perhaps new fields, and by taking good care to forget any retrograde movement, or any abandonment of old fields, that each fresh epoch imagines itself an advance upon those that have preceded it. How, for instance, do we plume ourselves upon our vast superiority over all that has gone before! How do we especially make merry over those dark ages whose blindness we fancy is in such striking contrast with the sharp-sightedness of these latter days upon which we have fallen! With what unction do we not dwell upon the unproductive labors of the subtle, hair-splitting schoolman of mediæval times, and how do we ever burn incense to ourselves in pitying the miserable recluse, who, shut out from the world, fell a victim to bigotry, asceticism, and superstition, and who, for all the good that his eyes did him, might have been, if indeed in our estimation he was not, as blind as the leathern-winged bat that in the twilight flitted about his mouldy, moss-covered monastery!

That the schoolman and the hermit have had their day, with small danger, and small desire too, of their restoration, and that their lives are in strong contrast with anything this nineteenth century can exhibit, is all true enough. But suppose one of those, as we esteem them, deluded, labor-wasting schoolmen, as Scotus or Aquinas, or one of those hooded monks, as Benedict or Bernard, could to-day, between the hours of ten and three, make his appearance on Wall Street. Would their strange costume and abstracted mien attract the gaze of the curious, gaping multitude, and would that be the end of it? Would nineteenth century activity and consequential bustle stand aloof, eyeing scornfully the unwelcome intruders, and would Young America, who so loves to air his broadcloth, shrink from the contaminating touch, and would that be all? Or rather would there not be there exhibited, standing erect upon the pavement, a character which would in some particulars tower head and shoulders above anything about it; a character whose solidity of material, whose disdain of sensual indulgence, whose ruggedness of temper, whose angular, sharply-defined outline, would stand out in bold and to some extent in grateful relief amid the effeminate, collapsed, voluptuous forms by which it would be surrounded; a character, indeed, having but small hold upon our sympathy, but cold and repulsive like the iceberg, and yet, like the iceberg, a something not to be greatly jostled by the small craft about it, — a character which, if not godlike, would at least make a sufficient approximation to the sublime to rebuke into reverence and admiration the thick throng that threads the thrifty thoroughfare, and to outweigh in point of solid worth a whole herd of the riffraff who swarm wherever the sugary sweet attracts them?

And further than this, should one of these strange visitors enter one of our gas-lighted halls, where some one of the many social schemes of the day is being discussed, even there their insignificance might not be altogether apparent; and any distinction attempted to be drawn in favor of the modern reformer, who would have all Johns and all Peters elevated at once into philosophers over those ancient devotees who inquired wherein the Johnity or the Peterity of the said John and Peter consisted, might be more difficult than we are apt to imagine. And, indeed, passing from the hermit to the alchemist, we might ask, without getting a ready answer, by what right do we, who aim at such transmutations as those just named, make light of that former experimenter whom we accuse of wasting his days in search of the wonderful elixir, or philosopher's stone, by which the baser metals should be converted into gold? If the estimate is to be based upon the results in the respective cases, it is barely possible that the experimenter in metals was as usefully employed as is his modern imitator who deals in more spiritual wares.

Is the reader beginning to suspect that all this is only a disguised sneer, a covert fling, at everything modern? He greatly mistakes my meaning if he falls into such a belief. Leaving any question of comparative excellence out of sight, as regards these opposite types of civilization, it is evident to everybody that the prevailing type of these days is not monachism, nor any of its belongings. We may have gained by the exchange; we doubtless have gained. But so, too, we have lost, for this is the inevitable law; and if it be a loss to which we give but small heed, that only proves our loss to be the greater. If we set small store by that severe spiritual and mental culture; that scorn of mere sensual gratification; that stern subjection of passion to principle; that rigid conformity of the life without to the faith within; that heroic self-denial which showed itself most, though not entirely, in passive endurance,—I say if we set small store by these virtues which the monastic state so strongly exemplifies, it only the more appears how the onesidedness of these days is not that of a former period, but something very different.

And suppose a little only of that olden spirit were infused by some miracle or otherwise into our own body-politic, how much that is now corpse-like would be quickened into life! How many channels now dry and dusty would be replenished; how many whose sullen, sluggish flow is now scarce distinguishable, would leap with a newborn vigor; and how, as is sometimes sought to be effected in the healing art by the infusion of healthy blood into diseased and stagnant veins, would the whole body-politic renew its youth!

The thought I am suggesting might be still

further elucidated by a reference to two of the most active and most powerful elements that belong to man's nature, and which have exerted an influence over the march of human events second to none whatever: I mean Imagination, and its yoke-fellow, Superstition. How both of these find subsistence in the earlier stages of society, and how they both struggle for a doubtful existence in an older, less heroic, more artificial age, is too evident to need remark here. If superstition or ignorance is the mother of Devotion, so some degree of mystery is the mother of Reverence. But mystery disappears before the light of an advancing civilization, and is succeeded by the familiarity which breeds contempt, and by a spirit of insubordination which always and of necessity gets to itself birth the moment no higher source of authority is recognized than that which man himself furnishes. Thus intellectual progress, and every advance in knowledge, is had at the expense of reverence, — an emotion which, as will be noticed hereafter, is quite as important to man, for the practical fruits which it yields, as Love itself.

There are few expressions oftener upon our lips than this, "The Spirit of the Age," and yet it may fairly be doubted whether there is one whose full significance we so little understand and appreciate. It is for the most part spoken of as being favorable or unfavorable to this or that interest, and so to be in turn either encouraged or resisted;

or it is resorted to as a convenient subterfuge or expedient, when we desire to find explanation for certain results whose causes we have not just then time to explore, or a gloss for certain equivocal events, whose justification we have not then and there time to attempt. But that it is often an absolute condition precedent to the success of a strict logical argument, whose value, as would seem, ought to depend on its intrinsic merits; that a purely intellectual process of thought ever yields fruit or is barren, according as the spirit of the age happens or not to be appropriate to its then introduction; that it may ever be properly likened, in its mode of operation and in its effects, to the flux sometimes resorted to by the metallurgist who desires to bring about the fusion of obstinate substances, — this, I suspect, is seldom considered. But, as I shall have occasion to notice elsewhere, the time when is an equivalent; a certain necessary adjustment of circumstances, or a preliminary preparation of soul, having always preceded great changes or epochs in the world's belief; great truths falling to our possession only when their "appropriate civilization dawns," — an expression for which I am indebted to Mr. Lecky, who, in his very instructive and suggestive treatise, "Rationalism in Europe," has elaborated this thought at considerable length, and has fortified his argument by the following very striking passage from Michelet, the historian, who is quoted as follows: "If the archæologist can determine the date of a monument from the form of its capital, with much greater certainty can the psychological historian assign to a specific period a moral fact, a predominating passion, or a mode of thought, and can pronounce it to have been impossible in the ages that preceded or that followed. In the chronology of art, the same forms have been sometimes reproduced, but in the moral life such a recurrence is impossible; its conceptions are fixed in their eternal place in the fatality of time."

Mr. Macaulay has figuratively described civilization as an ebb and flow, claiming for it a tidal motion like that which belongs to the ocean. The figure might perhaps have been carried still further, and so, without modifying, might have added to, the lesson it is designed and calculated to convey. As the ocean in its restless swell disintegrates, and with gnawing tooth gradually devours the rocky barriers which limit and restrain it, the outline of its shores thus undergoing a slow but constant fluctuation, so in the ceaseless, unquiet action of society, and in the restlessness of human thought, the boundaries of truth are subject to a somewhat similar change. Ancient beacon lights erected along the shore are suffered to expire; old forts, once guarded with religious care as affording protection to certain entrances, are dismantled and abandoned; and various newly opened inlets invite approach and exploration, which were formerly unknown or inaccessible. But as the ocean thus encroaches upon unaccustomed territory, and so in one direction enlarges its domain, it does this only upon terms of relinquishing some portion of its possessions elsewhere. So in like manner, as man advances with successive strides in the subjugation of new forces to his control, in the elaboration of new thoughts and new systems, and in the appropriation of new elements to his service, he is ever compelled to make some surrender of the "Old," which, if it be inferior to the "New," has still a value. Such is the law of Antithetical Equivalents: it bestows with one hand, it reclaims with the other. An amphibious life is not for man. For him there is nothing absolute. He shall make his choice, and having made it, he shall not be permitted to amend his prayer.

CHAPTER VIII.

THE FINELY MODULATED SCALE OF EQUIVALENTS.

If not absolutely the identical, it is one of the most prominent features belonging to this law, and one to which it owes no small part of its significance, that Equivalents are often weighed in much nicer and more sensitive scales than our careless observation would lead us to infer. We are ready enough to take account of, and to admit into our estimates, whatever is calculated to affect our grosser sense; whatever by its mere bulk, bigness, or outward demonstration of any sort, noisily declares itself, and vociferously asserts its own perogatives; whatever captivates our imaginations by mere pomp or dazzle. And so, too, of glaring mistakes or blunders men fall into, and of certain stereotyped, universally received causes of failure, either of omission or commission,— these we are always ready enough to pitch upon; and no sooner does an enterprise collapse, or some acquaintance of ours meet with discomfiture, than there are always ready at hand certain sage philosophers, with a gift of prophecy, who, had they but been applied to, could have easily foretold the event from the beginning; or certain plethoric, gushing demonstrators, who will set you down the why and the wherefore of the failure with a beautiful accuracy, — the reason and whole explanation thereof being drawn forth from some conveniently contrived pigeon-hole apparatus in their minds, where these reasons and explanations, alphabetically or otherwise arranged, patiently wait their turn for service.

Nor need it be denied that the pigeon-hole arrangement in many cases, perhaps a majority, works passably well, and under some letter or another in the alphabet of causes, most men by searching may find what suits their case. "The man has mistaken his calling," — this explanation is made to do very frequent service, being indeed almost always summoned whenever the appropriateness of others is too palpably wanting. And sometimes doubtless it is sufficiently near the truth, perhaps is the whole truth. Many men do fail for no other reason than this, and in doing so, illustrate the Law of Equivalents, since, being confessedly men of force, and so having in their hands the price of certain gifts, they fail to realize their advantage by a misapplication of their energies. And, as just remarked, they thus furnish an illustration of the law in its grosser and more palpable application. But it runs into much nicer shades than this, and is found extending into subdivisions of the same profession. Nothing, for instance, is more common than to find men of literary tastes and pursuits devoting themselves for years without success to certain branches of their profession, who afterwards achieve a brilliant reputation by hitting upon the precise vein which their aptitudes fitted them to explore. The light always belonged to them, but it was a light whose illuminating power was for a single path only. Their genius could be better compared to the ring of Gyges, which possessed but a single property, than to the lamp of Aladdin, which summoned not one but many genii to the aid of its possessor.

How, for instance, is this finely modulated scale of Equivalents revealed to us in the life of Charles Lamb, whose earlier literary attempts in other directions proving abortive, he, after an interval of twenty odd years devoted to ledgers and accounts at the India House, stumbled at last, as the phrase goes, upon the "Essay," and so outranks all competitors in that line since time began! How might the world put on sackcloth and ashes to-day had such a loss happened to it, and how easily might it have happened! And there are very many similar cases, if not full parallels; the only reason why there are not more brought home to our observation being, that life is too short for many men to find out, by "stumbling" or otherwise, what is the identical path for their genius.

Another instance of the kind, in some respects more notable even than that of "Elia," is furnished in the life of Samuel Richardson, the author of "Pamela" and "Clarissa." Having lived his life, as he seems to have supposed, for more than half a century, printing and publishing other men's thoughts, — having during this time got for himself a "respectable" name as a patient, plodding contributor towards supplying certain necessities of the world, and having thus settled it that he had no more lived in vain than has the man who raises potatoes or other esculents for the dear public, — the question at last occurs to him in a certain dim way, "Why not write and print and publish some of Samuel Richardson's own thoughts?"

And here is what Rousseau has to say about him. Speaking of "Clarissa," he says: "I yet remember with delight the first time it came into my hands. I was in the country. How deliciously I was affected! At every moment I saw my happiness diminished by a page. I then experienced the same sensations they feel who have long lived with one they love, and are on the point of separation. At the close of the work, I seemed to remain deserted."

And the encyclopædiacal Diderot thus discourses on the same subject: "O Richardson! thou singular genius in my eyes! thou shalt form my reading in all time. If, forced by sharp necessity, my friend falls into indigence; if the mediocrity of my fortune is not sufficient to bestow on my children the necessary cares for their education, I will sell my books, but thou shalt remain, — yes, thou shalt rest in the same class with Moses,

Homer, Euripides, and Sophocles, to be read alternately." And much more to the same effect.

And lest the reader should suppose these encomiums were in part owing to the comparative rarity of such books in those days, and that Richardson's claims have suffered eclipse by the appearance of subsequent competitors, here is what has been said of him within a few months by one of the most distinguished critics of the day : —

"He had been respectable, and helpful, and friendly from his cradle. One of Fielding's biographers declares contemptuously that Richardson had 'never known the want of a guinea, or committed an act which the most rigid moralist could censure.' It seems the worst accusation that could be brought against him. Neither man nor maid could lay their scath to him. He was a little fussy, a little particular, more than a little vain, but only with that simple vanity which is fed by domestic incense. None of those irregularities which are supposed to belong to genius existed in this homely man. He was diligent in business, plodding even, to all appearance, with a quick eye for his interest, and a soul capable of the most tradesmanlike punctuality and industry. He paid his way, built houses and barns, wrote and spoke a great deal of good-humored twaddle, and had not one spark of the light which so often leads astray, in his commonplace countenance. And yet, strangely enough, when the late blossom came, it was not a humble specimen of a class already known, but something entirely new and original. Had the world been aware that a new development of art was about to come into being, and that it lay between Richardson and Fielding to produce it, who could have for a moment hesitated as to which should be the founder of the new school? . . .

"From all the confused events of which the world was full — bewildering destruction of the old, still more bewildering formation of the new — the spectator turns aside into the quaintest homely quiet, the most domestic, least emotional of all household scenes, and there finds Samuel Richardson, — a good printer, a comfortable, affectionate, fatherly tradesman, kind to everybody about him, and very much applauded by his admiring friends, but with no special marks of genius that any one can see. Other men of far greater personal note breathed the same air with this active, pottering, and virtuous *bourgeois* — men with good blood in their veins and gold lace on their coats, and Greek and Latin at their fingers' ends, not to speak of youth, and vivacity, and high spirits, and a knowledge of the world. There was Henry Fielding, for instance, writing bad plays, and casting painfully about what to do with his genius. What was he to do with it? having at the same time an ailing wife and little children, burdens which Pegasus can take lightly *en croupe*, when he is aware what he is about, and has his course clear before him, but terrible drawbacks to the stumbling steed which is seeking a path for itself across the untrodden ways. . . .

"A more remarkable book has never been written; and when the character of the author, and his age, and all the circumstances that have just been described, are taken into consideration, the reader cannot but feel that the production is unique in literature. . . .

"The conception stands by itself amid all the conceptions of genius. No Greek, no Italian, no English poet, has painted such a figure in the great picture-gallery which is common to the world."

"How it came about that a homely soul like that of Richardson, amid the flutter of his pretty, fresh companions, — the girls that frequented his gardens like so many doves, — could have fallen upon the tragic ideal, is a very different matter. . . .

"We repeat, and with all the strength of conviction, that the highest poetic creation of the age is this one matchless figure."

Another instance hardly less remarkable is that of the painter, William Hogarth, who, having long struggled in the lanes and labyrinths of perplexed mediocrity, at the age of thirty-five emerged into a splendor which has suffered little diminution during the century and a half that has elapsed since he gave to the world the greatest moral lessons that the canvas has yet produced.

And so the list might be greatly extended,—this nice adjustment of brain, this delicate division of intellectual force, illustrating forcibly upon what minute and sensitively balanced points Equivalents often depend. The same thought has come under more general notice in speaking of the typical differences between the sexes, and, did my limits permit, might be still more particularly elucidated in this connection. The conversational powers of women have become proverbial long ago, and how, too, they excel in other departments, which are founded upon similar elements of character to those which support that gift, has been often remarked upon. Says the writer and critic already quoted in this chapter: " Women are very badly educated, everybody says, and everybody has said it from the remotest antiquity, and it is very wrong indeed that such a state of affairs should continue to go on as it has gone for several thousand years; and therefore it is most right and just to institute ladies' colleges, and courses of lectures, and university examinations. But yet the fact is that, so far as talk is concerned, the sisters of the boy upon whom we are spending heaps of money at Eton and Oxford are not only much pleasanter to talk to, but very much more ready and better qualified in many instances to take a part in those mild intellectual encounters, those little incursions over the borders of metaphysics, discussions of motives, sentiments, cases of conscience, points of social honor, which are the most prolific subjects of conversation, than not only their brother, but their brother's tutor, and all the learned community to which he belongs."

This is very well put, and fully recognizes this nicely discriminating Law of Equivalents; since neither the educational apparatus congregated at Eton or Oxford, or at Cambridge or Yale on this side the water, has ever been able so to equip the sons of these several institutions with that grace in evolutions, that skill in fence, or that adroit manœuvring in skirmishing encounters, which the "sisters" of these sons so naturally and so uniformly exhibit.

Style in composition affords still further illustration of this delicately modulated scale of Equivalents. This, indeed, is only a necessary corollary from what has been already a little dimly suggested. If style is the man — and who questions it? — then personality belongs to it no less than to man himself; and as no thought or sentiment dwells in the mind of two individuals under precisely the same form, or with the same identical significance, so, too, the form under which it is exhibited must likewise differ; until it happens that the manner of saying a thing, often signifies quite as much as the thing said, — indeed, seems to be a part of it. And in the same connection it might be observed, how a translation from one language into another, from an absolute necessity, fails to translate into the reader's mind the full meaning of the original; and this is all the more true, just in proportion as that original has a distinct value and distinct ear-marks of its own; the delicate aroma which belongs to it inevitably escaping to some extent in the very act of the transfer. Thus no man ignorant of the language in which it was written can ever pay the Equivalent for a full and perfect understanding and reception of "Faust"; perhaps it would not be altogether extravagant to say, that no acquired knowledge of that language by anybody but a native would suffice for this purpose.

The views here offered might be almost indefinitely extended; nor is it believed that they would be found incapable of yielding many practical lessons, were this the place to produce them. Among others would be this very evident one, — that more diligent inquisition should be made into men's or rather children's special aptitudes or affinities than the promiscuous methods of education now in vogue at all afford. It is surely desirable that some other process than "stumbling" should be hit upon, by which such aptitudes and affinities may be consulted, developed, and provided for. The practice, now become almost or quite universal in our colleges and seminaries of learning, of allowing elective studies, may contribute something towards this end; and whether these institutions have it in their power to do anything more than this in that direction, falls not within the scope of these pages to discuss. As remarked elsewhere, it is probable that the family must be chiefly depended upon for this result.

But at the risk of wearying the reader by the oft repetition, I must beg leave once more to remind him, that the present design seeks rather to demonstrate and illustrate a law than to hunt out the lessons which flow from it. And if in those instances which from their simplicity more readily reward our analysis of them, we find evidence that there is such a law, — if the further we pursue the investigation we still find cumulative evidence to the same purpose, — there surely arises a very strong presumption that the same law holds in other instances, where, owing to their more intricate, perhaps mysterious nature, we are less able to trace its operation. Said once a philosophical thinker: "Let me make the songs for a people, and I care not who makes their laws," — a remark which, well considered, involves a general truth of much more value than the particular one it was designed to convey.

CHAPTER IX.

UNCONSCIOUS PAYMENTS.

As in many particulars the Law I am illustrating seems rigorous even to cruelty, so on the other hand there is much of an opposite nature, and among the rest this, — that, if the payment be once fairly made, even though unwittingly by ourselves, we shall not fail of the reward. The statement as here made may seem to carry nothing with it very wonderful, — nothing, perhaps, to justify the making of it. And yet, if we will but put ourselves to the trouble of considering how very much there is everywhere else which is not unconsciously but all too consciously paid, — paid with tears; paid with sighing; paid with aching labor and wasting anxiety; paid with remorse and a broken reputation; paid with the very life-blood of the heart, that never gets reward, — the statement may not prove to be so empty as it at first seemed. After going through such a review, we should perhaps conclude it were worth something to hear of payments so certain to receive a return, that it happens to us without demand of ours, — happens to us although we were ignorant that we had earned even a claim to it.

And a very interesting and instructive page would it be, had we time and space to collect here the many exemplifications of this point which history furnishes. The disciple in the school of affliction and tribulation, the patient worker whose schemes are frustrated, and whose long matured plans, and fondly cherished hopes through a series of years, are crowned with disappointment, until in the bitterness of his anguish he exclaims, "All these things are against me," and implores Death to come to his deliverance, — not unfrequently finds in the end he has been all along paying Equivalents that yield him a sweeter and more abundant harvest than he had ever dreamed of. This is oftener true than the world ever gets knowledge of. We read the outside only of men's lives, while of that process and that experience going on within — those conflicts, those wrestlings, those agonies — we know nothing.

It may be thought that the allusion here is to certain results of a moral and spiritual nature only. But while it is doubtless true, that the principle I am speaking of has special application here, it does not stop here. If we always knew the history of purely material enterprises, and the preparatory discipline of deferred hope and patient struggling under disappointment which belong to that history, we should be surprised to learn how often these were the conditional contingents, the friendly forcing-house, out of which, and by means of which, the matured fruit at last gratified the patient worker. Some of the greatest and most valuable contributions to science and literature the world has ever received, have been at the hands of those who, through and by a long period of discipline and trial, have been making payments, all unconsciously, for the conditions of success; all the more grateful to them when reached, because for a time they were ignorant how their credit account had been all along improving at Nature's banking-house: while the Micawbers who have been slothfully waiting for something to turn up have leave to wait on, and wait forever; for slothful, querulous waiting is an Equivalent for nothing, — certainly nothing but disgraceful discomfiture, and a forlorn nakedness. Had Milton not been stricken with blindness, the greatest epic in the language might never have been written. Had Dante never been exiled, and had the current of his life always run smoothly, the world might have lost one of its greatest treasures, and the poet have failed of his immortality. From within the walls of the dark cell, and through the bars of the gloomy dungeon, has issued a light to shed undying radiance upon paths that else would have remained unknown and untravelled. Sir Walter Raleigh, Bunyan, Cervantes, Voltaire, De Foe, besides many others, will occur to the reader as familiar instances of imprisoned worthies, whose memories the world will not let die. So the child of sorrow often entertains a guest who in his flight leaves behind a fragrance distilled from no plant that grows in grosser soils. The victim of bitter disappointment and hope deferred, sometimes at least, finds that in these very thwartings which seemed too grievous to be borne he has been making payment for something that could come to him in no other way, but which he receives at last as abundant recompense; while

—— "the whips and scorn of time,
The oppressor's wrong, the proud man's contumely,
The pangs of despis'd love, the law's delays,
The insolence of office, and the spurns
That patient merit of the unworthy takes,"

are often Equivalents paid by the sufferer, which in due time yield their reward.

CHAPTER X.

NO EQUIVALENT FOR CONTENTMENT.

An Equivalent in the sense I am using the term implies something foreordained and established by fixed law beyond the possibility of change. We understand perfectly how personal experience is the one unalterable price for very much that is valuable. The fond father or mother would gladly, at what not sacrifice, introduce their child to the possession of certain truths by a less rugged and painful path. But they know how vain are all their efforts for such a purpose; they know that for this school there is no substitute.

And among the many lessons men derive from this source, there is one especially which they are very slow to learn even here. Temperament, of course, has much to do in determining the question of time, but for the great majority many years pass away, reaching up in some cases to the very meridian of life, and possibly beyond it, before the truth is fully accepted that, among the numerous Equivalents provided by Nature to be by us appropriated, she includes none for Contentment. She makes no such promise, — holds out no such pretence. And yet it is doubtful whether the united testimony of all who have ever lived has sufficed, in the absence of its own experience to that effect, to convince a single mind of this truth. "Man never is, but always to be blest,"—how does the buoyant elasticity of youth spurn the doctrine; how does each new-comer on the stage of life flatter himself that he shall furnish the exception to the rule! The trifling annoyances which surround the earlier years of life are plainly capable of a remedy and almost uniformly find it. So that green spot in the desert shall not prove for him a deceptive mirage, but a genuine oasis, where his feverish thirst shall be satisfied. This present state of dependence and vassalage will terminate; these days of drudgery will cease; these frowns of fortune will not last forever; obstacles will vanish before a resolute will; success, renown, shall wait upon the honest endeavor; and with these shall come that satisfied, contented spirit which is to reward all the toil, all the patience, all the sacrifice, of the past. These uneasy, querulous yearnings for something beyond shall cease; this aching void shall be filled, — this is the language, this is the hope, that, for the time at least, abides in the heart of every man.

But Nature makes no such covenant with her children while they remain tenants of earth. She says to us, to every one of us, no matter in what particular channel we may have directed our energies: "You have offered Equivalents for certain gifts, — professional eminence, power, wealth, luxurious indulgence, or what not. But the price you have paid was for certain specific objects. Those objects you have received. The price you have paid is exhausted, and those clamorous desires, those restless longings, that reaching forth of the soul for something that shall satisfy it, — all these remain as they were. You have failed to offer any Equivalent to be delivered from them, because there is no such Equivalent." And, indeed, so true is all this found to be, that the more we insist upon finding it, the more direct and specific our search for it, the more exacting and impatient our demand for it, so much the more it eludes our grasp. Nor does it matter in what particular direction, or under what form of self-abnegation, we endeavor to seek it out and appropriate it. The tumult and the stirring activity of city life, and the tame, quiet seclusion of the hermit's cell, alike refuse to yield it up on any demand of ours. We may range the whole domain of Nature, exhaust all her secret stores, and penetrate into her mysteries, and still our search shall not be rewarded with success.

And it is worthy of notice, that there is not only no Equivalent for Contentment, but it seems also that the identical sources which the imagination suggests as coming nearest to supply this vacuum are, on the contrary, farthest removed from it. Wealth, power, notoriety, luxurious ease, — in some or all of these men count upon finding the object of their search. And yet it is not unfrequently the case that the man who has these in the greatest abundance is the really discontented man. Every fountain of enjoyment open for him, he turns away disgusted with them all, and oppressed with languor and ennui he falls a victim at last to the very elements upon which he had founded his hopes. It is quite certain that many a man having all these sources open to him has been far less contented than have others who were without them, and that, if there were any Equivalent for Contentment, it would have to be sought for at the opposite pole from that where it is for the most part supposed to lie. Most of us learn this at some time. The "content of the cottage" becomes proverbial, but even this rests, in great measure certainly, upon a sort of poetic license; and so far as it does exist, is rather to be attributed to the sluggishness of desire, which is the normal result of a lack of culture, than to anything else in the situation; and perhaps those sensibilities which rest chiefly upon the impressions of early years are never more rudely shocked than when, upon entering this "lowly cot" expecting to find a quite divine content, we are met with upbraidings because our benefactions are not more regular, or are made to listen to an arraignment of Providence on account of his unequal distribution of this world's goods.

I have thus, as the reader will perceive, treated this point in accordance with the popular sentiment on the subject,— that men desire and aim at contentment. I doubt if this is strictly true. It can hardly be ranked among the desires. Men seek riches, or honor, or power, or sensual pleasure, not because these objects are recommended, by any supposed fitness belonging to them, to produce contentment, but partly in obedience to that principle of activity which is a part of their nature, and partly from a necessity which life imposes; but most of all under the promptings of certain clamorous appetites and desires, which find their gratification in the possession of such objects. To gratify a ruling passion, either natural or an artificial substitute; to banish ennui, that great foe to peace of mind; to be occupied and not idle; to make a part of, contribute towards, and identify themselves with, the movements of the world about them; to make life as much as possible a reality, and as little as possible a cheat; to cling to the illusions of childhood, and keep the heart fresh and young against the hardening influences of time and circumstance; to love and to be loved; to respect others, and in turn be respected of them,— these are what the great mass of men set their hearts upon; but of reaching a state of contentment by any or all of these avenues, very few, I imagine, ever think at all. Instead of saying that men desire to reach this state, it would be more correct to say that they are willing to accept it provided that in thus accepting it they are not hindered in their pursuits, thwarted in their plans, or restricted in their pleasures. .

The uses that are made of this subject are mainly two,— ethical and theological. Under the head first named, we are constantly admonished not to follow a certain class of objects too eagerly, or to set too high a value upon them, since it is not in their nature to produce content; but if men do not desire content, the argument would seem to be but poorly adapted to the purpose for which it is used. The theological view includes the idea just named, and so invites men to give their affections to a class of objects supposed to be more satisfying in their nature; but it also extends the argument still further, and argues a future state of existence, because these insatiable longings indicate certain attributes as belonging to the soul, which would seem to have been created to no purpose, unless better provision be made for them than is found in this world.

But there is a point intimately connected with the subject under discussion that suggests another question, which presents the foregoing argument under a modified form. And the question is this, — whether the absence of a desire to find relief against these importunate, irritating, disturbing appetites and passions does not indicate an incompleteness, an unfinished state as belonging to the soul, since it so readily accepts, and so freely acquiesces in, what seems so directly at war with its own peace and its own prosperity? Those clamorous, uneasy longings of which it is the subject, for something it never attains to, nor can attain to, in this life, doubtless convey very strong hints that it is hereafter to emerge into a different life and a different experience: but quite over and above this thought is that other, — that, as at present constituted and exhibited, the soul, instead of repelling and warring against this disease which so tortures and cripples it, rather invites and cherishes it; that is to say, it deliberately chooses to be a victim to these tempestuous desires, rather than to escape from them. Analogy, it is often said, is not argument, and that may be true enough, and yet it may be quite as valuable, certainly as efficacious, as are many of the arguments men set such store by. And in matters which do not admit of demonstrative proof, this instrument is always conceded to be very serviceable, if not indispensable.

Now, belonging to everything else except the soul of man, we find a self-assertive, self-rectifying, self-protecting element, — a something which is known as the *vis medicatrix naturæ*, which resents and opposes whatever is unfriendly to its own prosperity, or, if I may substitute the word, to its own happiness. The body, for instance, is no sooner injured, than it sets about repairing itself, and restoring itself from the effects of such injury,

NO EQUIVALENT FOR CONTENTMENT. 161

not unfrequently, indeed, finding its enemy in this soul which occupies it. A wounded tree, or a neglected or oppressed plant, is seen making every effort to heal itself in one case, and to atone for the neglect in the other. And so confident are we that a plant or an animal will uniformly do this, that we consider it dead, or very near the point of dissolution, when it no longer manifests this desire. Nor when it dies does there seem anything incongruous in its thus ceasing to exist, since, by thus having desired and elected what was for its highest good, it has given evidence of having reached a complete and finished state.

And such a manifest propriety does there seem to be, not to say necessity, that plants or animals, having certain functions to perform, should be constituted with a knowledge of what is good or bad for them, and then furthermore with a desire for the first and a rejecting of the latter, that we feel that nothing else than this is indeed the law which has been given them. It seems little less than impossible, if not absolutely impossible, it seems a palpable contradiction, to say that a plant or an animal should have been denied this knowledge, or should have been left without this desire; and nothing would surprise us more than to find a tree rejecting those elements within its reach which are friendly to its growth, and choosing those which are hostile to it. We perceive at once that, were this the arrangement, neither plants nor animals could live their life; we feel that, under the existing arrangement, they do live their life. And accordingly when children, who remain in an initial condition of weakness and ignorance longer than other animals, are found doing this identical thing, — that is, choosing what is not good for them, — we say at once that this is only an initial state, and that when they are old enough they will know and choose better. And, so, indeed as to many things this proves to be true, while however there still remains very much as to which this never becomes true, that is, in the present life.

Here, then, it is that we seem to have an exception presented to the above remarks; we seem to have found one instance in which the thing itself discloses as belonging to it a desire for that which it at the same time knows is hostile to itself, — of a thing which does not desire its own prosperity and happiness so much as it desires that which is opposed to both. That is to say, we find, not children, but the soul of man himself, deliberately choosing that which it knows will separate it from its own highest condition, its true interests, and its real prosperity; we find that part of man's nature, which we profess to believe is by far the noblest and most important part, denied this attribute which, as we have seen above, has been bestowed upon the inferior parts, and upon many other far less valuable objects. And hence it seems to follow, either that we err in thus assigning greater value to the soul, or that it at present only occupies an initial, incomplete state, which is to be succeeded by another when this disabling law in regard to it shall be repealed.

The same thought is capable of being pursued by a somewhat different process more closely connected with the general subject.

The theory which that subject seeks to illustrate includes within it this sentiment, — that, upon the presentation of an Equivalent, the reward inevitably follows, — that it must follow, because such a result flows from a connection established by a law of Nature. It hence follows that, in all cases of failure or disappointment, we are justified in saying that the full Equivalent has not been presented. This full Equivalent, as we have seen already, may not be, in the great majority of cases it is not, a single, homogeneous payment, but is made up of very many separate items, the withholding of any one of which items will be fatal, even though all the others have been produced. Even so apparently unimportant a point as the time when an enterprise is undertaken, may enter into the composition of an Equivalent, and success shall be substituted for failure upon making a change in this single respect only. The world is full of such instances. We constantly hear of men born out of time; of men and of systems, which are in advance of the age, or behind the age. We every day find ourselves saying in explanation of certain failures, the times are not yet ripe.

And in the main, men do not differ as to whether the Equivalent has been satisfied by being followed by a sufficient return. They speak of a misapplied, or miscontrived and so wasted, expenditure. And in the field of human industry, they always expect instances of such misapplication and miscontrivance. They expect failure; they count upon disappointment. They understand beforehand that much will be offered by man, which in his estimation is an Equivalent, which the result will demonstrate not to have been so.

But as to Nature's operations, they reason very differently. They never suspect her of making such mistake. They never feel concerned lest she should offer something as an Equivalent, which in the end will prove not to have been so. And if the reward does not follow the payment of the Equivalent by Nature as soon as they expected, they still confidently wait for it.

Now man's life on this earth is one of these Equivalents which Nature furnishes. And were the question put, whether it has been followed by adequate and suitable return, by a return proportioned to the expenditure, I think the answer would be uniform that it has not. For what could be accepted as a sufficient return? Among perhaps many other things, this certainly,—that man should be himself happy, as we speak of a tree being "happy" when it is in a condition of prosperous growth; and that he should at least be found desiring, if not fully capable of reaching, a point of contentment. Surely we must pronounce that the Equivalent which man's life furnishes is not followed by adequate return so long as that life lacks this element of happiness or prosperity to which everything about him attains, and especially when it is seen not even desiring a state of contentment, or at any rate is seen smothering all such desire in favor of other desires whose gratification is injurious to him; so that here at last seems to have been found one instance in which Nature herself has been disappointed.

And perhaps it is to escape from this dilemma, and find explanation for a fact which thus stands by itself, and contradicts all their experience elsewhere, that men so constantly flatter themselves with the hope of a "better time coming," when this seeming solecism shall cease. That is to say, inasmuch as they have in other instances found that time was a solvent of the difficulty, so they try to make the same explanation a solvent of the difficulty here; and they seem to imagine they have succeeded, if they can only demonstrate a change for the better in the near future.

But even were it demonstrated that from henceforth this Equivalent which man's life offers shall receive its due return, and so not prove any longer a failure, that cannot alter the facts as to those who have lived in the past. As to them an Equivalent has been paid which has been disappointed of its return, so that as to them we seem shut up to the single explanation we resort to in other cases where failure attends an Equivalent offered by Nature, and so must conclude in this case, as in those, that the time has not yet arrived. And inasmuch as for those who have lived in the past the time never can arrive in this present state of being it must happen, if at all, in another and a future state, and hence comes the deduction that there is such a future state.

CHAPTER XI.

HUMBLE CONTRIBUTIONS TO BE ACCEPTED IN CERTAIN DEPARTMENTS.

THAT very unequal degrees of success reward our efforts and attend our researches, according as they are severally directed to different departments of knowledge, is evident to all. "To him that hath shall be given still more abundantly," seems to be a truth as applicable to certain branches of inquiry to which men direct their attention, as it is to man himself. For while a certain class of subjects exhibit a steady, uninterrupted progress, at once grateful and inspiring to the investigator himself, and abounding in rich practical fruits to the world, there are others of an opposite nature, which are attended by very unlike results; their growth being not only slow, but being moreover incapable of that exact measurement which most men are so desirous of applying to the result of their labors.

And this inequality is chargeable to a twofold reason. There is a large class of objects which so naturally captivate our imaginations, both by yielding fruits of a kind that we highly prize, and by yielding them, too, at little or no risk, that we neither require incentives in our search for them, nor have we much occasion to thank those who make their acquisition more easy by new discoveries. They are quite able to take care of themselves, and fall into our hands by a process not unlike that of gravitation.

On the other hand, there is another class differing from this one in both these particulars: they for the most part fail to commend themselves to our highest regard, and the laws which pertain to them are less easily understood; our energy in pursuit of them being thus hindered both by lukewarm emotions, and by uneasy questionings as to whether our labor shall meet with certain reward. There is no greater impediment in the way of steady, successful exertion than doubt, for doubt and enthusiasm are sworn enemies. But the class of objects I am now speaking of is surrounded with mystery. They defy our most earnest attempts at analysis; they elude our most searching investigations. After patient following of tedious and perplexed paths, the explorer returns as empty as he went out, his chagrin by no means diminished as he is made to behold the abundant harvest that falls to the lot of others, who have entered into more propitious fields.

And to this department belongs, first, everything that involves the principle of life. Busied with only inorganic substances, having to do with objects that he may weigh, and handle, and taste, and measure, the chemist pursues his inquiries with a certainty that leaves no room for misgivings; with accessions to his knowledge ever new, to inspire ever new ardor, to encourage ever new hopes. The stepping-stones which lay behind him are visibly there, each having its own little flagstaff erected upon it to show its exact significance. The shore he is exploring has its many sinuosities, intricate perhaps, but they are sinuosities walled about with rock that fears small change from the elements of storm or tide, and once described upon his chart, they remain there for future reference; while the ever-changing course of a rushing stream between banks of an alluvial formation is an apt emblem of his labors who seeks to penetrate and drag into light the almost inscrutable mysteries which envelop every living organism. The diagram and the field-notes of this year must be reconsidered and amended the next by additions here and deductions there, the very changeableness which characterizes the track already passed giving constant and disheartening intimation of the futility that shall attend his future explorations.

Thus, wherever the principle of life is found, there mystery begins,— there any rapid advance is not to be looked for. Involving this principle are the two sciences, Medicine and Agriculture; and although perhaps no two can be named to which a greater amount of attention has been devoted, there are no two that have remained so nearly stationary. Since the discovery by Harvey, early in the seventeenth century, of the circulation of the blood, no signal advance has been made in the science first named, unless we except certain improvements in surgery, and the employment of anæsthetic agents, which last is doubtless of very considerable advantage in relieving pain, and in rendering critical operations less hazardous. But this can hardly be claimed as an exception to what is here asserted, if indeed it does not rather confirm it. For even with the important aid furnished by the use of these agents, I am not aware that any more thorough knowledge of diseases, or of the cures that are applicable to them, has been reached, than existed before this discovery was made known. Nor, as we survey the various competing systems now in vogue, does there seem any greater likelihood than formerly that any one of them should succeed in establishing its own supremacy.

So in the other science of Agriculture, which has to do with vegetable life; the absence of any great improvement is still more noticeable. The carelessness and want of accuracy which almost uniformly characterize the experiments of explorers in this field might be assigned, perhaps, in part explanation of the failure: but this very carelessness is itself to be attributed in great measure to the want of faith in any results; a want of faith, too, which arises out of this identical unapproachable nature of the objects to be investigated already suggested. And, too, among the points belonging to this profession which still remain in dispute, many seem simple enough. If the potato disease could not expect to find ready explanation and cure, we should suppose the young practitioner might not unreasonably expect to be referred to some authority which would definitively assure him whether small seed be or be not as profitable to plant as large seed. Nor would it seem very exacting if the new beginner should count upon being informed, upon inquiry to that effect, how large a proportion of its substance a plant derives from the soil, and how much from the atmosphere; or that the question of fertilizers, their modes and time of application, the depth to which they should be covered, their value as proportioned to their cost, and other like points, should have been at least approximately determined. And yet there is not one of these points that is not often mooted as doubtful. And as remarked above, the doubt which invests this whole subject, and which refuses to yield to investigation, arises from the fact that wherever there is life — a living, growing organism — there is also mystery. The laws that regulate its growth are incapable of being fully penetrated.

But again. Other departments are equally obstinate, and refuse to yield a large return, not so much from any mystery that pertains to them as from the almost infinite number of objects they include, the variegated and capricious character of those objects, and the immensity of the field over which they are scattered. To understand the relations which objects such as these hold to each other, and then to predict a single and a certain result, or arrive at any infallible mode of treatment, is beyond the wit of man. The science of "Political Economy" is an instance in point. It makes but little and very uncertain advance. The treatise by Adam Smith, published in the last quarter of the eighteenth century, contains as much that is true, and as little that is false, as anything that the world has since received at other hands. Cognizant as this science is of objects upon the earth, it is far less certainly understood than are the laws that control the heavenly bodies which are millions of miles away. The return of a comet may be safely predicted within a few days, or even hours, but no man can tell us with certainty when to expect a crisis in financial circles. Such a question includes altogether too many and too capricious data to give any value to predictions of this kind; for the character of a season, as hot or cold, or wet or dry, a favorable or unfavorable harvest time, and a multitude of other influences still less capable of being grasped by man, overthrow the most carefully prepared calculations.

Again: all inquiries which fall under the head

of "Mental Science," termed metaphysical, or what not, are still more proverbial for their unsatisfactory, contradictory results. Interminable discussions, and the laborious researches of the highest scholarship, give us little but antagonistic theories and systems, out of which the uninitiated disciple must select such material, and form for himself such conclusion, as he may. But here it is unnecessary to enlarge.

Now, in all the above-cited instances, the world has long since ceased to expect any approach to certainty, or to look for any very decided strides in advance of the old positions. It has signified its willingness to receive very slender contributions, so that they be real; since the class of subjects here indicated, by their very nature, preclude the possibility of that accurate analysis and that intimate knowledge which are the conditions of richer gifts. The Equivalents have not been placed within our reach, offering which, we might be justified in looking for something better.

But there is one Science which to a very considerable extent is burdened with all the difficulties above enumerated as belonging to many and different departments: I mean the "Science of Society," or, as it is generally termed, "Social Science." In the first place, it is to all intents and purposes a living organism. It involves the principle of life; just as everything else does which gets its increase by growth, and not by making.

This difficulty, therefore, it must encounter at the very threshold. In the next place, far more than Political Economy, it includes within itself not only a vast number of objects, which are scattered over an immense area, but these objects are exceedingly variegated in their nature, and, what is more than all the rest, they are shifting and capricious beyond what we find anywhere else. To extract from the experience of the past any reliable estimates which shall serve as fixed data upon which to found our calculations, to arrive at anything like the experimental knowledge we attain to in certain other branches of inquiry, is totally impossible. The calculations of to-day are overthrown by unexpected facts of to-morrow. Accidents, as we term them, of blight and frost, come to scatter the blossoms which gave early promise of abundant fruit; or, to change the figure, we are, by some unconsidered trifle, switched off upon a track whose divergence we had little suspected, but which lands us at a point quite wide of that we had contemplated.

And finally this Science of Society has to contend with the same vagueness of outline, the same lubricity of touch and delicacy of texture, the same twilight obscurity and mystery, which belong to metaphysical science. The laws that pertain to it and regulate it are beyond our grasp. The almost infinite variety of theories that have been advanced respecting it, and the innumerable nostrums that from time to time have been offered to meet its demands, alike testify that the problem is incapable of anything like a final solution.

And seeing that this is all true beyond question of any man, it is not a little surprising that the world still refuses to abide by conclusions as to this " Science of Society " which, upon similar but less abundant premises, it long ago consented to accept as final everywhere else but here. In other departments, as remarked above, it signifies its willingness to accept what its own observation and its own experience demonstrate to be possible for it, however little such possibility may include. It asks no magnificent contribution; it is content to take but little, because a little is evidently all it can get. But when it comes to this " Science of Society," which has to contend with accumulated disabilities; to a science which embodies in itself the several obstacles to progress that belong to all other sciences put together; to a science in whose discussion a greater contrariety of opinion has been disclosed than we find almost anywhere else, — when it comes to this, the world not only demands, but sometimes seems to think it is on the point of receiving, nothing less than the veritable specific which is to cure all its maladies and remove all its weaknesses. The philosopher's stone for the transmutation of baser metals into gold is only remembered as proving our own superiority to such daydreams; while our faith in certain other transmutations is as strong as ever, and our pursuit of them as fervid as it was before innumerable disappointments had proved that pursuit to be as vain in its results as it has been absurd in its premises.

Does the question arise as to any possible antidote for all this misleading charlatanism, — all this beguiling, seductive romance? Are we fain to rid ourselves of a weakness which seems to give the lie to that boasted intelligence which is supposed to be peculiar to this nineteenth century? Should the claim be set up that the particular law here attempted to be illustrated furnishes such antidote, it might perhaps not unnaturally be retorted that that would still be charlatanry, similar in kind to that here brought into judgment, and differing from it only in form; since it presupposes an acceptance of and a resort to the pretended remedy as conditions of its being effectual, which can by no means be confidently counted upon. Not, perhaps, an altogether unfair criticism, and yet, still bearing in mind that it is a question of the elevation of humanity, could it once be known how far an acknowledged advance in this particular may be traced to an increased attention directed, in these later days upon which we have fallen, to the supply of material or bodily wants; to the bettering of man's external condition by such contributions as are indicated by the multiplication of charitable institutions in all their diversified forms, even his spiritual wants sharing indirectly in the fruits thus gathered, — it might suggest the inquiry whether all this may not have been in fact owing, in part at least, to a more full recognition of this identical Law of Equivalents, new colorable support being thus found in its behalf. For if the Law have only this credit allotted to it, it ought surely to be content, since, by the very terms of the subject now in hand, it is not only admitted but asserted, that humble contributions are to be thankfully accepted in certain departments, since these alone are possible.

CHAPTER XII.

VARIEGATED SOURCES OF CIVILIZATION.

CIVILIZATION, in its wide sweep and all-embracing comprehensiveness, — in its manifold requirements, and its voracious rather than fastidious appetite, — includes all Equivalents of what name or degree soever. Even the vices, and infirmities, and grossness of men offer to it no small contribution; the very machinery devised for the punishment of offenders, — courts of justice and their ministers, the jail and the penitentiary, the detective police, the sheriff in the performance of the saddest office that falls to his lot, — all these bring no small accession to the grand result.

And they do this not only in the more palpable sense of preventing crime and protecting life and property, but, striking upon the surface of society at points which would otherwise remain undisturbed and unruffled, they create new centres of life and activity which without them would be unknown, and so help, as do all separate and distinct agencies, to prevent the mere routine, and the mechanical, automatic movement, to which society itself tends. They help to make it many-sided; to keep alive a faith which under old civilizations degenerates into mere habit; to give point to conviction and a living energy to the heart of man, which otherwise would be exchanged for careless acquiescence or indiscriminating indifference.

Thus, paradox as it may seem, civilization draws part of its sustenance from the very evils that afflict, the very dangers that threaten it. If all men should become honest and should learn to settle their own disputes, and rogues should be converted into virtuous men, both the magistrate and the priest — the sanctuaries of religion and the temples of justice, and those who minister at their respective altars — might be dispensed with. All the mental activity of which these are now the occasion, all the variegated contributions they now bestow upon society, would at once be lost to us, upon the necessity of them, and so themselves, disappearing. Somewhat in the same way as Mother Earth absorbs again into her bosom the decay and the refuse of animal and vegetable life, and so, removing out of our sight what is noxious and offensive, returns it to us again under new forms of beauty and of profit, her failing powers being thus reinvigorated and her fruitfulness restored, is civilization itself in part kept alive and advanced by the very enemies it has to contend with; civilization itself, by its capacity of conversion and assimilation, out of decay and unsightliness, bringing forth both flowers and fruit whose absence we should at once be made to feel and deplore.

The more evident sense in which society depends upon and flourishes by the luxurious and extravagant, and even vicious, habits and indulgences of its members, needs here only a passing allusion. By far the greater part of the revenues of the three most civilized nations now living are drawn from tobacco and spirituous liquors, both of which, if we may believe the different writers on the subject, are the prolific source of mischief to the consumers of them. So, too, most of the more innocent luxuries of life for the gratification of appetite, and the costly apparel which the tyrannical laws of fashion and the love of ostentation invite, are not only gathered from far distant points, thus laying the foundations of commerce, with all its ramified extensions and diversified stimulants, but they furnish employment for myriads of idle hands, and assist in the distribution of that wealth which ever tends to great centres; just as, by evaporation and subsequent condensation, water is taken up from its grand reservoirs, and returned and distributed in the fructifying rains and the refreshing dews of heaven; the stagnant, putrefying marsh affording as pure a source for these gifts as does the transparent lake, or the surface of the living, ever-moving ocean.

Some of these reflections, we are aware, are trite enough, and they are introduced here only as belonging to the general subject. They illustrate, and exhibit at a new angle of observation, the law we are considering; and they especially admonish us to search out the so-called humbler instruments and sources of progress, since, if we are so greatly indebted to these impure sources, those that are not resting under such stain, even if the stain of humbleness do belong to them, ought to find a new recommendation in our eyes. If Nature does not scorn to bestow upon us, and we do not scorn to receive at her hands, advantages through base and contaminated channels, it would seem we should not so soon forget our own helplessness and insignificance thus indicated to us as to refuse to employ channels which are subject only to the single charge that they are not pretentious and magnificent.

CHAPTER XIII.

SOME UNIVERSAL EQUIVALENTS — TIME.

It seems not out of place here to notice cursorily certain Equivalents which, being always insisted upon, may be termed universal, in distinction from others of a more limited and variable application. And first, Time, both time when, and time how long.

The time when, — how very much depends upon that! Nothing perhaps would bring this home to our perception more clearly than to consider the half century that has just closed, and to estimate the change that even that short space of time has sufficed to produce in men's minds on great fundamental points of belief. Truths which announced fifty years ago would have been rejected as extravagant whimsies or fatal heresies, have now passed into the very web and woof of men's belief; and arguments which would then have been worthless, because very few could have been found to listen to or appreciate them, are worthless now because very few are so unenlightened as to need them. Perhaps, indeed, the same thought would find more striking illustration by selecting a still shorter period, and a careful comparison of public sentiment as it now exists, with what it was on many subjects previous to the late civil war, would disclose a change which has reconciled men to very much they then recoiled from, and has rendered possible certain theories, and given success to arguments, which would then have perished in their very utterance. So in times of commotion, and under the excitement of stirring events, when old fetters are melted away, and thought is set free from its former keepers, it takes to itself new forms and new features, and men rapidly lapse away from their old belief. The time arrives, the past receives its sentence and goes out banished forever, and the new becomes not only possible, but inevitable.

And taking a wider survey, where the sweep of the glass includes within its horizon the past history of the world, nothing is more forcibly revealed to our notice than the fact that a certain preparation to the minds of men is necessary before a particular truth or class of truths may be received. Says a modern writer already quoted: "Each epoch, each different phase of civilization, has its peculiar and congenial views of the system and government of the universe, to which the men of that time will gravitate; and although a revelation, or a great effort of human genius, may for a time emancipate them from the conditions of the age, the pressure of surrounding influences will soon reassert its sway, and the truths that are unsuited to the times will remain inoperative till their appropriate civilization has dawned." In the course of the great changes which happen to men's belief, it is not only that Truth widens her circumference, and so enlarges her domain, but what is quite as important, new centres are formed, with their respective powers of attraction, and when these are once established, the rest is easy and follows as matter of course. As an intricate piece of machinery, in its advance towards perfection, receives at the proper hour new accessions which at an earlier period would have been useless, and therefore not suggested, so it is with new truths. Very much is accepted without effort by one generation which a former one rejected, although no new argument has appeared in its support. A new level of intelligence, or a higher plane of vision, has been reached, or the emotional part of our nature has been remoulded, until both our reason and our sympathies consent to that which, in a preceding age, seemed only a pernicious heresy. The Inquisition imprisoned Galileo, when he announced his great discovery, not because the argument was deficient, but because they supposed it contradicted a theologic dogma. So, as has been seen already, the belief in witchcraft disappeared, not when some abler opponent came to attack it and unmask its weakness, but when the time arrived for a clearer vision, and for more correct sympathies to teach its folly.

Thus, if the "prosperity of a jest lies in the ear of him that hears it," with still greater truth may it be said, that the success of an argument depends upon the mental and emotional development of those to whom it is addressed. Humiliating and discouraging as may be the admission, there seems not a little to support it, that the greater the necessity for argument, — greater either on account of the magnitude of the evil to be removed, or on account of the prevalent stolidity of the public conscience in regard to it, — the less is the likelihood of its being immediately successful. The very conversion of sentiment we seek to produce, seems to be a condition precedent to the appreciation of the argument. The mind very seldom yields its assent, however conclusive the reasoning, while the sympathies remain in opposition. But these take their color, at least on all questions of a public nature, from long accredited habits and modes of thought; and until the hour arrives when a general revolution takes place in public sentiment, the forms and processes of logic avail but little. As Mr. Lecky has remarked, in a period of the world when bull-baiting was in accordance with the prevailing taste, any opposition to such an amusement, however skilfully put, would have been utterly wasted. So, under the system of slavery as it recently existed in the Southern States, — a system having the conscientious approbation of the entire community, — no representation of its real or supposed enormity could by any possibility have produced conviction in minds preoccupied by an opposite opinion, or have overthrown sympathies which had long entrenched themselves in the deepest recesses of the heart. There are very many topics which might be brought with profit to the notice of an American audience, with reasonable ground for hope of good results, that, presented to our friends of the Celestial Empire, would produce no impression whatever.

So, too, in glancing over the history of individual nations, we are forcibly impressed by the very irregular, intermittent, capricious march of civilization; and in the different degrees of impressibility and intellectual life which mark the different stages, we see again how the time when, becomes an important element. Epochs of fruitfulness and barrenness, of activity and torpor, follow each other at unequal distances. The Augustan age, the times of Leo X., of Louis XIV., and of Elizabeth, stand forth in marked conspicuity, bright spots in strong contrast with the periods that precede or follow them. The hummocking process, described by Dr. Kane in his account of the exploring expedition which he conducted, affords an illustration in point. At one time everything seems locked in the embrace of death, no signs of vitality or force anywhere; vast fields of ice, stretching as far as the eye can reach, present to the view one unbroken level, one sterile waste, one all-pervading silence, as though the world were just finished and had not yet begun to move. One would as soon look for fruit or flower in a sepulchre, or energy beneath a shroud, as for evidence of life there. But presently, coming one knows not whence, beginning one knows not where, there are incipient signs of vitality. A mysterious force is being generated, soon to assert its inconceivable power, and to attest the presence of a living agent even there, where a moment before seemed to be only the repose and the torpor of death. An almost imperceptible convexity is first discovered on that level surface. Slowly but steadily it swells its dimensions, and now the entire field seems endowed with frightful energies, all which are concentrated on that central point. Still the pinching process goes on, the convexity rapidly increases, until at length immense blocks, or rather obelisks, are forced first slantwise, then erect, from this strange quarry, and the result is, in Arctic phraseology, a hummock, — in other words, an Egyptian pyramid in ruins.

In a somewhat similar manner great changes happen to society, and when they happen bring the appointed time, the fit opportunity, which very often constitutes the Equivalent whose absence is not to be excused.

And time how long, — that, too, is oftener insisted upon as the inevitable price than at all suits our impatience, or accords with our theories and our reasonings. We plant the tree to-day; we would gather the fruit to-morrow. Frequently reminded as we are, how very much that is of real value comes to our hands only as a product of growth, which in the nature of it requires time, and hence does not admit of being hurried, whatever the costly bribe may be that is presented, we still wonder at Nature's delay to recognize our offering, and repine because, notwithstanding our zeal and our self-sacrifice, the world is not made better in a day. Time being the true Equivalent, we seek to gain our end by a substituted price, and purchase into our possession what no man ever yet received for himself or accomplished for another, except by the one appointed channel, that is to say, of growth, of development, of protracted watchfulness, of careful observation, of patient culture.

CHAPTER XIV.

THOUGHT.

It would be a great omission not to include thought among these universal Equivalents. In the true sense of the word, it is the one most seldom paid. It may seem only an affected paradox to say so, but just as there is much believed, and yet very little belief, so we may say there is much thinking and but little thought. There is, for instance, a kind of delicious reverie, in which many habitually indulge, which they term thinking; but this bears about the same relation to downright, earnest thought, that the dalliance of the amateur gardener bears to the severe labor of the sturdy husbandman.

Nor can the reading of other men's thoughts, although they be good thoughts, with any more justice be styled thinking. Indeed, the multiplicity of books, and the facility altogether of obtaining matter to read, is often remarked upon, and very properly, as most unfavorable to this exercise.

But, what may seem less evident to some persons, hard and severe study is not necessarily thinking. Just as a man may, with a cormorant appetite, devour whole libraries and never devote an hour to thought, so he may be a laborious student all his life and never have given a single day to this process. Nor will any knowledge he gains of his own powers, by the success that attends his studies, be of use in deciding what his power of thinking may have been, nor what point he might have attained to in that department. Some men can think who cannot study, and some can study who cannot think. They are distinct exercises, quite as much so as is the operation of balancing distinct from that of leaping, and what a man can do in one of these operations is no test as to what he can do in the other. He may fail in this and succeed in that. So a man who has never put the matter to the test of experiment has no means of knowing what his power of thought is, — how much thinking force belongs to him. The fact that he has never practised thinking does not of necessity imply that the latent power of doing so is not there present.

And it seems not unnatural to suppose that a greater amount of latent force has been thrown away just here than almost anywhere else, and merely because men have assumed that it did not belong to them. There is certainly no one thing men so generally neglect, and a strong presumption arises, to say the least, that, had they brought this faculty into action, as they do their other faculties, the results would be at once manifest. But while other mental exercises stand well enough in our estimation, and receive a fair share of attention, for some reason or other thinking — I mean downright, earnest, severe thinking — is neither practised nor esteemed.

And one reason for this is, our not being apprised of how much we are capable in that direction. Few men ever make the experiment fairly. They allow their thoughts to flit hither and thither, not considering that it is an incubating process, and that the same subject must be brooded over for many months, perhaps years. Goethe's "Faust" was in his mind, drawing to it rich juices, almost a lifetime before it was born; but once born, it shall now live forever. Then a subject must be selected in which we are interested, either naturally or by bestowing care and pains upon it, so that the emotions shall supply the necessary warmth. Others are discouraged because the fruits do not at once appear. They forget that it is a stepping-stone process; and just as a man in looking at a complicated piece of machinery has a sense of his weakness, since he feels how impossible it would be for him to contrive such a machine, and just as this sense arises in great part from his not reflecting through how many successive steps it has advanced to its present perfection, so many a man judges his power of thought. Because he cannot leap at once by a single bound to the object, he straightway pronounces it beyond his reach. Other men can think, but not he. But more than anything else, thought proceeds step by step, inch by inch, through a long series, and like the drifting sand of the desert patiently heaps itself against mighty systems and pyramids of error, until, proudly and defiantly as they raise their crests towards heaven, they are at last buried forever out of our sight.

But what is meant by thought, so that I am correct in saying there is little of it? Men doubtless think in their various occupations and professions; they think about their families and their pleasures. As a people, it is a charge brought against us, that we overwork the brain by imposing upon it too much thought. But the kind of thought here spoken of is something men use as a means of attaining certain personally remunerative ends, just as they use a locomotive to bear themselves or their commodities from one point to another. With them it is an instrument to forward material enterprises — to assist mere secular pursuits. Even the man who is engaged in some one of the callings supposed to make particular draft upon the intellect is not necessarily a man of thought in the sense I am now using the word, any more than he whose pursuits are of a less intellectual nature. He for the most part only subsidizes thought to work out a certain purpose, professional or otherwise. It is for him a sort of Swiss mercenary, to fight a battle or win a cause for him. The truth it discloses must be such truth as suits his purpose.

The blows it delivers must be on the side which his interest or prejudice has preordained to be the right side.

Nor need it be denied that even such thought is an Equivalent for very much that could never be had without it. But when it is spoken of as one of the universal Equivalents, a process is intended very different from all this. And as just now hinted, it is not a process subordinated to bring about with more or less violence a specific result, or trammelled by prejudice in favor of a preconceived dogma or theory. There is plenty of this subsidized thought in the world, which perhaps quite as often confirms and establishes error as it reveals and fortifies truth. Instead of this, it is more a tentative, experimental process, rather to be likened to the explorations of Columbus, who aims at the discovery of a new and unknown continent, than to the voyage of the merchantman, who seeks a particular haven, and regards all winds and all currents as adverse that do not assist him thither. It is a letting the mind work, not setting it to work, in this or that rut; not so much giving it a set task to perform as receiving gratefully and modestly what gifts it has for us; not so much employing it as a servant as bowing before it in its capacity of lord.

Nor shall we be at all prepared to give thought its true claim to be classed among "Universal Equivalents" until we have in mind this free, catholic, independent thought here indicated. We must think of it, not as circumscribed and cramped by allegiance to systems, — biased and bribed by professional interest, warped and contracted by, and receiving color from, forms which crystallize about it under the ephemeral influences of a civilization which flowed to us to-day and is destined to flow away again from us to-morrow; not as confining its survey to, and forming its estimates from, that small portion of the stream which passes under its own immediate notice, — but we must think of it as something which, poising itself not too confidently in the present, extends its vision into the dim past and the remote future; as something which ever holds in remembrance how the great stream of causes and events never ceases in its flowing, and how theories as idolized and systems as accredited as any that we hold to-day have in their turn appeared and vanished; as something which never forgets how for man there is nothing absolute, and how the soul of man, with all the limitations which belong to it, as it has been in the past, so must continue to be in the future, both the source and the measure of his attainments.

How little the world knows of thought like this, need not be here remarked upon. Nor need it any more be remarked how it identically is one of those great primal, universal Equivalents which is the sole, inevitable, inexorable price for very much that is of incalculable value to man. The world may, indeed, grow without it and so become bigger.

The circle of knowledge may be widened, and made to include a greater variety of objects than have yet passed into man's possession; just as the astronomer, by a change not in the nature, but in the power, of his instruments, may enlarge his circle, and bring more remote bodies within the range of his vision. Nor is there any occasion for depreciating the value of labors like these, or of the gifts they have it in their power to bestow upon us. These, and labors like unto these, are Equivalents for growth, but it is by thought and by thought only that the world moves; all else, that only resembles motion and cheats us by its false pretences, being begotten of something very different. For real motion that shall never disappoint us, thought is the only Equivalent. To it, and to it alone, has been imparted a semblance of that Divine attribute which creates. And thought does create. It does not merely widen old circles, and amuse and glorify itself by forming and computing magnificent circumferences, but it creates new centres, towards which the mind of the world shall from thenceforth gravitate, and around which it shall from thenceforth revolve, — new centres, by which men shall thereafter take their "departures," and from which shall radiate beams of light and heat unseen and unfelt before. Such a new centre was furnished by Aristotle, and in later times by Bacon, who set the world a-spinning far to the right of that old rut of mouldy speculation and subtle refinings about essences and entities. Such a new centre was given by Luther, by John Wesley, and in a different department by Harvey, by Galileo, by Leibnitz, by Newton, by Adam Smith, by Watts, by Fulton, and others like them. But did these men get to themselves this inspiration, and this power to make the world move, by thumbing over other men's thoughts, and by newly contrived, cunning processes of manipulation? Never. And had no other Equivalents than such as these been forthcoming, the world would have reached a very different point on the track of progress from that it shows to-day.

Thought, then, is an Equivalent. It is better than money-giving; it is better than diplomacy; it is better than the shifts and the skirmishings of politics; it is better than sentimental aspirations; it is better than the laborious research of mere study; it is better than everything save one only, which one is Wisdom, and which is begotten itself of Thought and its handmaid Humility, the twin yoke-fellow of Thought, to whom and to whose fair progeny the world owes more to-day than it wots of, or at least more than it is always ready to acknowledge. Says Ralph W. Emerson in this strong language: "I hate this shallow Americanism, which hopes to get rich by credit, to get knowledge by raps on midnight tables, skill without study, mastery without apprenticeship, power through a packed jury or caucus, or wealth by fraud." I am inclined to think that Mr. Emerson believed in a Law of Equivalents.

CHAPTER XV.

PURITY.

SHOULD the question be put, "What is that thing which, next to certain great, universally recognized sources of wretchedness, such as crime, abject poverty, loss of friends, and the like, makes the most serious deduction from man's happiness?" unanimous answer were hardly to be expected. And should this answer be given, "Impurity is that thing," not only would assent be frequently withheld, but not seldom, I fear, the dissent would be attended with a sneer. And for two reasons: A coarse man is absolutely excluded from the very perception or power of realizing what purity means; and he either doubts its existence altogether, or it becomes, with him, only another name for effeminacy and insipidity. But, on the other hand, there is an opposite class who, setting the highest possible value upon this element, are moved to a degree of indignation and loathing at its affectation, which is proportioned to their high estimate of its genuine worth; but it does not always happen that the indignation, which was intended only for the counterfeit, is so interpreted. A certain stain is carried over to the thing itself, and purity is made seemingly to hold a lower place in the esteem of the world than really belongs to it. In giving expression to our hatred of prudery, we insensibly, but almost necessarily, allow the thought to overreach, and so bring a prejudice to the thing which is affected or imitated.

But notwithstanding these embarrassments which attend the question, and still more the discussion of it, it remains none the less true, that impurity not only shuts out the subject of it from the most refined and altogether most exquisite source of enjoyment open to man, but, to borrow a figure from medicine, it shocks and lowers the whole tone of the moral organism. The law which it violates is set as a guardian over a part of man's moral nature, more delicate, and sensitive to injury, and more difficult to be restored from the effects of such injury, than the eye itself; to which organ in the body it may be not inaptly compared in respect of its saving us from various pitfalls and dangers to which we are exposed. For, however the school of modern "Free-Lovers," and the whole tribe, their imitators, may sneer at this exhibition of the subject, and may set a light value upon the sacredness of the conjugal relation, it is for every people, and, for reasons I cannot here stop to explain in detail, especially for the American people to-day, one of the very highest and most important of all truths, that out of this relation, properly preserved, spring conservative influences,—

influences which extend far beyond individual life, and reach to the health of the state itself, which are second to none whatever. For, as I shall remark more at length hereafter, this element seems to hold that favorite place in Nature's estimate of it, that any injury done to it will be avenged by what in the legal profession are termed "exemplary damages."

In the treatment of this part of my subject, I have thus far rather played into the hands of the utilitarian class of philosophers, who insist that utility is the only foundation of virtue; for I have laid the chief stress upon that class of valuable fruits, which it places in our hands, that are bestowed upon us by others, and do not flow out of our own lives. But it may be worth while to inquire for a moment whether the subject is not capable of being turned to very different account.

As there are two classes of offences, — those which injure chiefly the individual who is guilty of them, and those which are hurtful to society, the last-named being held in much the deepest reprobation, — so there are two classes of virtues, to which the opposite distinction belongs. Men generally set a far higher value upon those virtues which affect directly their own comfort and security than they do upon those whose effects seem to be more confined to the individual who possesses them. Honesty, courage, generosity, public spirit,— these, and others like them, may be turned to account by the community in which they are found, and we accordingly find them held in high esteem, and always certain to receive full meed of approbation. Business integrity, as it is sometimes termed, — that is, a promptness and faithfulness in meeting commercial engagements, — this especially stands in high repute. And even those of inferior rank which fall under the head of accomplishments, such as politeness, affability, cordiality,— these also receive due share of praise.

And it is upon facts like these that the class of ethical writers above mentioned attempt to establish their system. According to their theory, men are not only attracted to virtue by reason of its being remunerative, but its utility is the only distinction which separates it from vice; any intrinsic excellence belonging to it, or any special authority it can lay claim to, being by them denied.

But there is one virtue at least — that now under consideration — to which no such external reward is attached, if indeed, as already remarked, the possession of it in an eminent degree be not sometimes regarded as matter for reproach. And although, speaking with absolute correctness, purity must rather be classed among the instincts than reckoned as a virtue or a principle, still it is so intimately allied to virtue, and so almost impossible is it for a pure-minded person to fall a victim to habitual viciousness, that the distinction can hardly be insisted upon; so that here, at least, if nowhere else, we may assert that virtue is attended with a reward simply as virtue. For surely it is from no prudent calculation of the profit of it, that we arrive at our estimate of its value to ourselves, or that we are induced to fashion our lives by its dictates. It does, indeed, as above insisted, bestow upon us not only rich, but also variegated rewards; but that portion of the reward which falls to us individually, at once ceases and wholly disappears unless we are attracted to it and practise it for its own sake. By a refined subtlety of reasoning, we may succeed in persuading ourselves that elsewhere virtue has no other foundation than utility. We may assert that what seems the most disinterested benevolence is to be traced back to some selfish motive, and that we exercise it only because we find that to do so, in various ways contributes to our own comfort. And so through the entire catalogue of virtues: ingenuity may resolve them all into a mere consideration of advantage to ourselves. But I think he must have attained to great address, not to say finesse, in reasoning, who can thus manipulate purity, and resolve it into a mere question of utility.

But to proceed. Purity being that element which contributes so largely to man's happiness, and being indeed the very condition upon which he may attain to the highest happiness of which he is at all capable, we are led to the inference that it is in a peculiar sense a law of his moral constitution; and that, while the infraction of certain other laws in the main affects prejudicially only those particular parts of his nature to which they severally belong, the infraction of this law gives a shock and conveys distemper to his whole nature. We assert of a piece of mechanism, that it has most nearly advanced to perfection when it best performs the particular office for which it was designed. And in like manner we should be justified in pronouncing man perfect if he were once perfectly happy; for that would show all unnecessary friction removed out of the way, each part acting in harmony with every other part, and the identical result which was intended, thereby absolutely secured,— to wit, his own happiness, since this, by the very terms of it, seems to imply perfection. Indeed, it is curious to observe how we sometimes feel, and take pleasure in feeling, that even a nonsentient, mere material object is "happy," as for instance a tree, when by its flourishing condition it announces that it is obeying its own law. And so perhaps it is owing to the same principle that by a certain extravagance of language we often speak of this or that well-working machinery as a "happy" contrivance.

And since purity is in itself, and without reference to any fruits it indirectly bestows upon us, a source of the very highest happiness, we may speak of it as the keystone in the moral arch, and so regard it as not only possessed of great value in itself and for its own sake, but we are almost irresistibly led to the conclusion that a certain precedence would be awarded to it as a helpful ally and coöperator in the pursuit and cultivation of other virtues. True, such efficacy belongs to a considerable extent to every virtue: it strengthens the whole family of which it is a member. Nay, more: even that which rises not to this dignity, but only resembles virtue, as for instance sensibility of soul, shall often be admitted to share with Virtue in her work, and so help to restrain the excess of evil passions, and the ascendency of hurtful vices, all this honor being thus accorded to it merely for this resemblance; the fact being, what we do not always perhaps sufficiently consider, that, but for his sensibility restraining him, many a man now quite innocent, if not indeed outwardly amiable, might have emulated the cruelty of a Nero or a Caligula.

I say, then, we might have inferred beforehand, even were the fact not attested by our observation, that purity would be specially signalized as a handmaid in the cause of virtue. But this fact is so attested, and that most abundantly. Nor am I willing that it should be robbed of any portion of its intrinsic value by its being associated with some particular system, and so its truth or importance be to some extent attributed to such system. Nothing hinders that an irreligious man, in the technical sense of that term, should be a man of pure heart and life; nor need any intellectual eccentricity, if that is the word, which opposes the reception of certain so called evangelical formulas, deter any man from the cultivation of purity, and making it the rule of his life. How far a technically religious life may be calculated to assist in such process, is quite aside from the present discussion; but to assert that the two things are naturally, and therefore necessarily, associated, would be both false and mischievous. Indeed, as has been intimated already, nothing is more certain than that men may often find themselves resting under a disqualification of a strictly intellectual nature to receive certain truths assumed to be such, and yet, possibly through suggestions of the heart, exhibit the practical fruits of such truths in their lives. As few men illustrate, in their daily walk and conversation, the full, logical results of a mere speculative belief, so, on the other hand, very few live up to their scepticism. An almost infinite variety of causes, lying quite outside of the circle of pure intellect, come in to twist and modulate men's actions; not only the thoughts and convictions of the most honest, careful, and independent investigator taking color, in spite of him, from the circumstances about him, but beyond all this, very much interposing between his convictions and his performances. It is quite likely that very many, both North and South, since the question on which they lately so differed has been settled, already find themselves receding somewhat from the positions they held when the discussion was at fever-heat; but even at the moment when it was raging in all its intensity, so much so that men were estimated solely by the stand they took in relation to it, only comparatively few, called fire-eaters at the South, and fanatics at the North, acted fully and at all times up to their convictions. These convictions, fortunately for the world, are with the vast majority always tempered by collateral considerations; the few more violent and more steadfast fanatics who remain, not without use, since they act as cog-wheels to prevent a too precipitate return to the dead level of indifferentism.

Seeing, then, that this twofold preëminence is awarded to purity,— first, that it is in itself the very highest source of happiness to its possessor, and is moreover a most serviceable ally in preserving and stimulating other virtues,— I think we are fully justified in the inference, even in the absence of our observation to that effect, that it would be an object of special care, and would be protected by special penalties, so that whoever should inflict injury upon it, either by direct violence, or transgression against it by his manner of life, would be made to feel the consequences of his error in a degree and with a certainty that does not attend a disobedience of laws which have not been exalted to so high a place. I think that Nature, having thus elevated purity into a representative virtue, would follow out her plan, and insist that this favoritism of hers should find response in men's conduct, and that impurity would be found to be indeed "that thing" which with special emphasis would make most serious deduction from their happiness.

And unless the foregoing remarks have no foundation to rest upon, it follows that a preëminent claim belongs to purity, to be classed among Equivalents. It has in a very marked degree all the attributes of an Equivalent. It admits of no substitute. There is nothing which even approximates an atonement for its absence. It is the price of rewards which can by no possibility fail upon the payment thereof. And perhaps I shall be pardoned by the reader if I remind him, once more, that the subject is introduced here primarily to illustrate the law, and not for the sake of the lesson which it teaches. For whatever value may attach to such lesson, in these pages it holds only a subordinate place; the real intent being to explain and enforce a general law, by whose reception and operation not purity only, but very much else besides, shall be elevated into its proper rank, and be recognized as of specific value.

CHAPTER XVI.

PERSONALITY.

IN speaking of Equivalents, it is impossible to omit from the enumeration the distinct personality which belongs to every individual. And I remark in the first place, that every man is a unit. Invited as we constantly are, by psychological writers, to survey man as compounded of various parts; grown familiar with a vast technical nomenclature which rests upon minute analysis, upon refined and subtle if not idle distinctions,—we talk now of the head, now of the heart; now of the soul, now of the intellect; of affections, emotions, passions, desires, instincts, the will, and the rest. We thus in a manner lose sight of the fact that every man is a distinct unit; the entire aggregate of forces which belong to him, of what name soever, however they may be surveyed separately and apart from each other, producing a single and a necessary result: no one of these forces ever for a moment to become inoperative, not one of them to be for an instant eliminated from the problem of his life. He is not man plus this or that desire or emotion, plus certain appetites or passions, plus intellect, plus will; but these are the man himself. When the man acts, each and every of them contributes more or less towards the character and complexion of that act. They are all present. We may not, indeed, always watch the process going on within us, so closely as to detect this entirety, this unity, this concert. And we may without impropriety speak of a man as being carried away by violent emotion, overcome by passion, misled by enthusiasm, held in check by a strong will, according as one or the other of these elements severally happens to hold a preponderating influence for the time. But we may be sure that the act, every act, when consummated, is a result of the whole, not of a part of him. Each and every distinct element may not have been consciously summoned to sit then and there in council, but the whole man's weight is in one scale or the other. No part is or can be set aside, and so its voice be silenced; no part can be banished into temporary exile, and so its influence be got rid of; nor, as I hope to remark more fully in another place, can one part suffer without injury to the whole. And as this is true of each single act, it is also true of the man's life. That life is the resulting product, indeed, of a complex mechanism; but complex as it is, it is a unit in its exercise and in its operation. And except so far as it is affected by accidents of the external, it is the result of nothing but this, — the result of a superintending law which takes note of him as a unit; a law which excludes accident, and provides for a single, inevitable result out of all this complexity. And so every man is an oracle, in a certain sense, for every other man, but not always rightly interpreted.

Again. Every man is not only a unit, but he is also an individual. This individualism may not always, it is true, be readily detected among the uncultivated class, and for this very reason we use the phrase, "the masses," when speaking of this class. We mass them in our estimate of them, because the culture which is necessary to bring out individual traits has in their case been wanting. But they are one and all no less individuals; each differing from every other, each having his own distinct personality. As he is a unit, and so no one of the various forces which enter into his composition is ever silent, so no one of them can by any possibility be put away or exchanged for another. "Which of you by taking thought can add one cubit to his stature," affirms a disability belonging to his spiritual nature, no less than to his body. Each and every man differs, and is made to differ, from every other man, all buying, all borrowing, all interchange as to natural lineaments absolutely and forever excluded.

Nor does anybody ever think of finding any fault with this view until, being committed to some system, or resting under some similar necessity, he is thus, as it were, bribed to do so. Nobody ever advises another man to be more talented, while almost every man has friends who recommend this or that change in his moral as opposed to his intellectual nature. "Why do you not have a little more energy?" — how often are we made to listen to that precious bit of advice! while we might as well say to the man on his way to prison for debt, "Why do you not have a little more money?" "Why be so sensitive?" "Why so fastidious?" "Why so timid?" "Why so over-modest?" How constantly are our ears saluted with questions of this kind! As well might the physician, who finds his patient suffering under a too nervous temperament, suggest to him to make an exchange, and so become more phlegmatic! As well ask Tom why he is not Harry, or Harry why he is not William! So, too, of the will: how do writers on these subjects continually speak of that as a something over and above the man himself, and he is gravely admonished to take that will of his in hand and fashion it over again, and it shall be the better for him! just as a man who finds himself the owner of an inconvenient or unprofitable piece of merchandise is advised to exchange it for something else; or as a heavier balance-wheel may be put into a piece of machinery if the one there already is too light.

This personality, then, cleaves to a man forever and at all times. To it he is bondman each day, every hour of his life, with no more power to separate himself from it than from the shadow that attends him. To the extent of its significance, it is the man's law. For individualism implies and includes law; is indeed little less than a synonym of law. But it is as absurd to speak of a man's escaping from the law that pertains to him as an individual as it would be to imagine that a vegetable or animal may be separated from the law which pertains to it. And while it is no part of my purpose to raise here the vexed question of man's freedom, or freedom of the will, it seems absolutely uncontradictable that, be his liberty more or less, it can never exceed that state in which he is left after all the demands of law have been satisfied. No atom in the material universe is made for itself alone, but with reference to its relations towards all other atoms. Nor can it be supposed anything less is true of man. His relations to others, and his own place in the moral universe, are fixed and immutable. If he is free to act, free to consider, free to choose, free to decide, it is still a freedom under law. Mere being, whether animate or inanimate, in the very nature of the case, is law. To offer proof that this or that thing or animal, or that this or that function, is a subject of law, is as superfluous as it would be to attempt to prove a mathematical axiom. For if a thing or an animal be an individual; if it cannot be in two places at once; if it cannot change itself into something else than it is; if it cannot at the same time be both hot and cold, a solid and a fluid, sick and in health; if it cannot have anything added to it, or taken away from it, without ceasing to be the thing or animal it was before; if, in fine, there is anything it has a power of doing and an incapacity of doing, — all this is law. Being is law; living is law.

And as to this personality which belongs to every man, it is worthy of remark that it is not confined to certain definitive powers or qualities; certain elements that may be catalogued, and labelled, and measured, and so by a mere description a complete knowledge of him be obtained, just as, by such a process, we get a knowledge of a country or a tree. True enough, we are not without such descriptions. There are biographers in plenty who, with measuring-tape in hand, are ready on the instant to set you down this or that distinguished individual, so much wit, so much imagination, so much quickness of perception, so much emotion, and all the rest, — estimates not destitute of interest, nor without value. But above and beyond all this there seems to be something which, so to speak, holds these qualities, something which, for want of a better comparison, may be likened to the setting of the lapidary. For in this particular, who ever found his curiosity satisfied by a biographical sketch, be the number of pages greater or less? It is not that the writer lacks honesty, or that he is swayed by prejudice or partiality. It is not that he has been denied sufficient "material," or that anything has been kept back from prudential considerations. The unsatisfactoriness of the picture is not owing to any such drawbacks as these; but we find ourselves always turning away from the text to the picture in the frontispiece, thinking thus to get some help towards penetrating the secret. And still more to the purpose is a sight of the man's living face, and better still an interview, if it be for only a few minutes. For with liberty to put such questions as we please, and have them answered, we make but little progress towards getting at the marrow of the subject.

Nor, indeed, when the personal interview happens to us, are we at any great pains to verify the previous description, nor does it occur to us at all to inquire whether the statements we have listened to were correct. These all vanish out of sight as irrelevant, no longer occupying our thoughts even; but once there in the man's presence, we find ourselves occupied with very different questions from any we ever put before; or rather the knowledge flows to us without any questions, and by a process it would puzzle us to describe. All those tape-measurements, those results reached by the aid of a spiritual goniometer which sets down with exemplary faithfulness each and every angle, — all these have taken flight, entering no more into the account.

I am not aware that any name has yet been found for this subtle essence. We might call it soul, but that word has been already appropriated. "Flavor of character," an expression lately made use of by some writer, is perhaps as near an approach to a definitive formula as the case admits of, the phrase itself indicating that we must taste for ourselves and not another for us. And how sometimes, notwithstanding the tenacity with which we cling to our own identity, quite resolute against exchanging it for any other whatever, does it occur to us that a temporary arrangement of the kind would be both pleasant and profitable! How by such a process, far better than by any other, should we be conducted to the evasive secret! How should we be at once informed as to the manner, by what light, by what springs, by what steps, another man's mind moves and arrives at certain results! We flatter ourselves that in this way we should be put upon the track of scenting out some weakness that belongs to us, and then apply the corrective. Then, too, we sometimes construct what seems to us a logical argument, but we often ask ourselves if it be not possible there is some other solvent, something outside of our logic, in another man's mind, which might modify our own conclusions. We are constantly made to see, too, in the case of others about us, how a certain obliquity of mental vision leads them into error, and at once suspecting that some similar defect may belong to ourselves, which has however escaped our search for it, this exchange of identity suggests itself as a very convenient, if not indeed the only, means by which we could be thus enlightened. But we understand very well how impossible is anything of this kind. We cannot even measure either the mental operations or states, or the emotional experiences, of another against our own. We have no means of knowing in what degree, for instance, a beautiful landscape, or fine poem, or other pleasing object, affects ourselves more or less agreeably than it does our friends. It would doubtless be very pleasant to have such means of comparison. Very pleasant indeed would it be if we could compare our own mental and moral and emotional processes with the corresponding processes which are common to those with whom we are associated. When we hear expressions of delight, or approbation, or censure, we are perhaps sensible of a concurrence in our own minds; but we are sometimes very strongly moved to know the degree in which these sentiments are held by our companions, but all this is quite beyond reach of ours; for, anxious as we may be to impart or to receive the secret, it abides with the owner of it as if there were no other person living.

And it is perhaps curious, if nothing more, to reflect how this individualism renders us, to the extent of it, sole proprietors of the universe. If no two persons are exactly alike, then every man includes something within himself which belongs to nobody else in the same proportions. And in so far as he differs from any and every other man, so far he comes into contact and communion with the world, and has a proprietorship in the world and all that it includes, which belongs to nobody but himself. And in this sense he is sole monarch. The starry heavens, the mysterious winds, the roar of ocean, the stillness of forest aisles, light and darkness, diffusive heat, all the inanimate universe, and the still deeper mysteries which belong to man's sentient nature, are in this sense his alone, just as certainly, though not in the same degree, as they would be his, if they were realized by him through a sixth sense which did not belong to those about him. Every beautiful poem, or other work of creative art, has a separate significance for him, in which no other person, not even its author, can share.

But some of these speculations are getting to be a little wide of the mark. All I aim to do in this chapter is, to bring the point into connection with the general train of thought I am seeking to illustrate. If there be any such thing as a Law of Equivalents, then it must extend to and include man himself, with all the complex mechanism, both bodily and spiritual, brain and heart, and body and soul, that belong to man. Each and every man is a separate Equivalent, to fill his appointed place, to make return of appointed results; and every other man than this, introduced by stratagem or stealth, if such a thing were possible, is only a derangement and an interruption of the great whole, which ceases to move by law, and hence also with certainty, the moment anything appears which is either above or without law.

And this being so, it follows that the one great, primal, paramount Equivalent for every man is his own personality. It is a grim, defiant wall, from the cradle to the grave separating him from every other man, giving him distinct joys, distinct sorrows, distinct triumphs, distinct disappointments, a whole distinct accountability, which can never belong to another, and which no other can ever fully understand or fairly interpret. The world comes into contact with him, and he comes into contact with the world, at points which can happen to no other man who has ever lived.

Brain, heart — intellect, emotion; how in the presence of these, as they belong to each individual man, are all other Equivalents dwarfed into merest pigmies; nay, how rather do they seem the two great original and originating Equivalents, all others being only their servitors, and hardly deserving the name at all; useful and effective only as they run their errands, as they execute their behests! But this brain, this heart, so much of each weighed out in nicer scales than the goldsmith's or the apothecary's as the separate portion of each individual man, — what an inexorable law of limitation, what minute carefulness of division, what seemingly unnecessary parsimony of distribution, and to our eyes not only unnecessary but wasteful and ill-considered, since, by a small withholding, so much that has been bestowed is rendered useless! Lived there ever a man yet who was not made to feel that only a hand's breadth beyond the borders of his own allotted territory, hanging over his head from tantalizing boughs almost within hand-grasp, were fruits almost his own, but still irrevocably never to become his own? How is he made to reflect that, had this fine network of his brain only been arranged a little differently, even with no greater strength belonging to it, he might have ensnared the subtle thought of which now he only catches the passing shadow; or how would he sometimes rejoice at what seems to him would be a most advantageous exchange, when he should receive but a little here for much more liberal surrender there! The wall that separates him from successful achievement so high, so impassable, and yet so thin,— thinner than the tenuity of the air-blown bubble; fruition many times more miles away than the remotest star, and yet almost audibly knocking at his heart, an infinitesimal millimeter of brain interposing and separating man from man and man from success, as whole continents do not separate them in space.

As already casually remarked, nowhere does this Law of Equivalents seem more rigorous or more cruel, or attended with greater evil and hardship to man. Nowhere is it so difficult to accept with resignation this Law as when ourselves or our friends are made to find honest, solid, substantial claims, which everybody acknowledges, set aside by reason of the presence therewith, or the absence therefrom, of what, measured by us, is utterly insignificant. Many practical lessons flow from considerations like these, but I can here mention but one of them: the whole subject inculcates charity as to moral delinquencies, and a lenient criticism as to intellectual blemishes. The State, it is true, by a necessity which belongs to the case, is forbidden, in her capacity as administrator of justice, to go behind overt acts; and only in certain exceptional cases, when the motive may be inquired into to determine the degree of criminality, or whether a crime has been committed at all, does she profess to look into the heart, or to take into account individual infirmities, whether hereditary or otherwise. And the example the State thus of necessity sets to the community is not unattended with mischief. For while men as individuals are under no such compulsion, and nothing forbids them to apply these extenuating circumstances, they are very apt to allow themselves to be invited to a similar undeviating rigor by the pattern which is so often placed before their eyes in the execution of penal law.

Nor need it be disguised that Society itself rests to a considerable extent under the same necessity which belongs to the State. For its own protection, it is for the most part compelled to judge men by their actions only. It shows small inclination, and indeed has little power, to inquire very carefully into heart secrets. But as between individuals, all this is changed; nor is much danger to be apprehended lest we should reach that laxity of judgment which would give undue encouragement to vicious or hurtful propensities. We may — to be just, we must — take into account individual peculiarities of intellectual and emotional organization; not, assuredly, to the extent of blotting out all distinctions, and condoning all offences, but to cause pleas in extenuation to be listened to, much oftener than is found to be true in the every-day manners of our life. Under the artificial and arbitrary forms of Society, there is enough of evil growing out of harsh judgments which there is no way of avoiding, and for which there is no antidote; and a more careful attention to the two great facts — that for man there is nothing absolute, and that every man's personality cleaves to him forever — would do much towards banishing from the world that extreme severity, and that promiscuousness of judgment, from which it now so suffers; there hardly ever being found a man who at some time in his life is not made to feel the necessity to himself of this considerate estimate.

CHAPTER XVII.

WOMAN SUFFRAGE.

THE doctrine asserted in these pages, and attempted to be enforced and illustrated, is that for a large class of objects a certain specific payment, or payment in kind, is exacted, to which I have given the name of Equivalents, which being withheld, the object in question can never become ours. No substituted price, be it ever so worthy, ever so magnificent, can ever be accepted.

If the proposition be true, then, to the extent of the truth embraced by it, it is a law. And if it is a law, it has a very direct bearing upon a question largely agitated in these days as to disturbing the present arrangement which limits the right of suffrage to man, and so excludes woman from any participation in the same. I propose to examine this question in the light of the truth I have been discussing, and to inquire what testimony it furnishes towards a correct solution.

And if Nature exacts a certain specific payment as the price of her gifts, the correlative of the proposition requires that she also furnish the specific, distinct source from whence that payment may be derived. One implies the other, else we should hear of equivalents for certain objects supposed to be attainable, while for such equivalents no provision had been made. If we have wandered and become lost in a labyrinth of error, and there be but the one Ariadneian thread, to wit, a retracing of our steps by the same way. we entered, by whose aid we may be restored to the freedom and blessedness of rectitude, and if at the same time we are given to understand that such escape is possible for us at all, then we infer with certainty that this identical thread has been provided and will reward our search for it; otherwise this Law of Equivalents is no law. If exercise be the sole condition upon which we may attain to strong muscular development, and if we are taught that such a development is within our reach, then we know that such exercise is possible for us, just as certainly as we know, certain pleasant fruits of the earth having been promised us, that the moisture, and other friendly elements necessary to the production of such fruit, will not be withheld.

And seeing that Nature thus sets certain gifts of hers against certain specific payment to be made by us, and seeing that, to get into our hands the power of making such specific payment, we are shut up to the sources severally provided and pointed out as the only sources, then it follows, so closely indeed as to seem a part of the law itself, that just in proportion as these sources are preserved to us in their original integrity and purity, just so far they retain their power for good without diminution; but, on the other hand, they lose something of that power whenever they are contaminated, and cease to have any power at all when, the real purpose for which they were originally contrived and designed being lost sight of, they are converted to foreign or perverted to illegitimate uses.

And we are admonished to abstain from any such intermeddling, or attempt at conversion of a given equivalent over to another than its own distinct use, when we consider upon what very nice and minute points such equivalents turn. In proportion as they are nice and minute, in the same proportion must they be respected and obeyed by us. As an example, wedded love is one of these sources. It is a channel through which equivalents flow to us second in value to no others whatever. But the moment it is despoiled of its purity, the moment its individual integrity which separates it from all other sources is broken in upon, that moment it is shorn of its power.

Again. We may imagine equivalents drawn from sources somewhat akin one to the other, so that the equivalents themselves they severally yield are not very widely distinguished one from the other; or we may on the other hand have in our mind quite an opposite class, where, the sources being very wide apart, and separated one from the other by many points of difference, indeed by their whole nature, the equivalents they severally furnish will in like manner be widely separated as to the nature of the gifts they are each capable of bestowing. And as to the comparative value of these two classes, it is quite evident that the one last mentioned is of far greater value to us than the other, because, if we are to be subjected to a loss at all, it is better to lose that whose absence is atoned for by something which remains nearly resembling it, than to lose that which, having belonging to it a singularity of value, its absence is less easily atoned for.

Requesting the reader to take along with him what has been thus premised, I proceed to inquire what bearing this law of equivalents has upon the subject in hand. Nowhere throughout the whole range of Nature do we find a broader distinction, or one more clearly marked, than is presented to our view in the difference of sex. Nowhere does it seem to have been the fixed design of Nature to bestow upon us a source of such diametrically opposite equivalents as is furnished to our hands under this arrangement. It will hardly be expected that I should here and now enter into a minute analysis of the existing distinctions. My object is rather to apply a law than to enter into any nice dissertation, and for the present I am not forbidden to assume as granted that such typical differences do exist. They are absolutely antipodal. To say that a man and a woman are equally capable of doing very many things, that they may often interchange occupations with each other without loss or detriment, in no wise militates with this assertion. Indeed, that they may do so, within certain limits, only serves to bring out into more bold relief the points which illustrate what I am now contending for.

And the other fact that man may with advantage sometimes borrow from woman, and so that epicene character be the result which is sometimes met with and always admired; or the converse, though not, I think, with equal truth, that woman may sometimes borrow from man, — is no more opposed to the view I am presenting. " Kiss me, Hardy," said the dying Nelson to his lieutenant, and who that witnessed the scene, or has only read of it, did not feel that to the emotional, feminine organization which this touching request betrayed, was to be attributed in part the gallant commander's success? The lives of very many men who have achieved great results might be cited to the same purpose. The gentle spirit is often the bravest, and he whose heart is the quickest to warm towards the weak, the helpless, and the injured is the very man to be relied on in the shock of battle; many a more rugged nature fleeing from the field while he remains to die there, or to redeem the desperate day and plant the standard of victory where lately was nothing but rout and defeat.

But this is no conversion or perversion of equivalents. The grafting of a tree, so that it is made to produce fruits not natural to it, is no conversion or perversion of the laws of Nature. On the contrary it is a striking and beautiful illustration in the material world of this identical law, that whole rugged and apparently intractable material of the old stock being subdued and turned into a channel not its own by the delicate scion there inserted; itself an equivalent, able to contend with and bring into subjection all that obstinacy of sturdy trunk, and all that wealth of far-spreading, fibrous root, to its own purpose, showing again how the less overcomes and is superior to the greater, and how the humble agent is often the efficient agent.

No more is there any conversion in the instance of Nelson cited above. Did anybody ever suppose that the wall of division which separates and distinguishes the sexes was in danger of being broken down and disappearing forever, because a man is sometimes found who in a degree beyond his fellows happens to partake of the nature of both sexes, or that the distinction is any less real, less founded in a great natural law? The truth is, that while the distinction exists in all the breadth I have claimed for it, there is very much common to both; nay, the distinction itself will be found to rest in a great measure, not in the possession of different qualities, but in the different degrees in which they are held by the two. But the distinction is none the less real, none the less important.

And perhaps nothing will more strongly incline us to admit the truth of this distinction than when we ask ourselves what are the contributions the two sexes offer to civilization. I say then, first, man acts, woman endures. She lets her light shine by that beautiful life of hers. We judge men, estimate men, by what they perform, frequently, it is true, falling into error by an excess in this particular: we estimate woman by what she is. Every properly constituted mind acknowledges that it is the highest glory of a woman to be a true woman. She may write fine poems, she may paint beautiful pictures, she may get to herself credit and reputation in other departments, and we may gratefully receive such gifts; but all this is only subordinate, only a something contributory to her first great claim upon our respect and regard. Says Milton, as quoted by Mr. Carlyle: "He who would write heroic poems must make his whole life a heroic poem." And such is the life of every true woman, a heroic poem in itself; and yet we are told she must vote, or the measure of her life is not filled.

She who is a true woman, lacking these brilliant endowments, far outranks that other, be her intellectual stature what it may, who is destitute of this real womanliness of character. There may not be, indeed for the most part there cannot be, such a public exhibition of it that the world at large shall take note of it; but if nothing is valuable but what will bear this test, great deduction must be made from former estimates. Nor am I inclined to make such a concession as that would be, should I admit that the argument requires me to define what is meant by womanliness of character. Every man, unless indeed he be incapable of the conception at all, understands its meaning perfectly well, without help from me. Every man, without entering into such families to make a particular observation, knows the difference which distinguishes one from the other, according as sons only, or both sons and daughters, severally belong to them, and I should feel perfectly safe in accepting the test as final and conclusive on the whole subject. The truth is, it is of altogether too delicate a nature to be subjected to a rude and inquisitive analysis, to be measured, and weighed, and branded, like a piece of merchandise. To admit any capacity of critical definition belonging to it would be to disparage its real value. For it does not consist in purity and gracefulness alone, or in a refined taste, in devotion to those she loves, in tenderness of heart, in delicacy of instinct, in quickness of perception, in intuitive knowledge of truth, in fortitude under suffering, in heroic self-sacrifice and lofty self-denial. These, indeed, are included in it, but they do not constitute it. When some one will tell me in set, formal phrase, wherein the silence of the forest differs from that of the ocean, and that of the hushed city at midnight differs from them both, I will tell him in definitive phrase what is meant by the womanliness of woman.

Now unless all this is false, there is furnished to us here one of those great, primary sources which is capable of yielding certain equivalents that otherwise may not come into our hands at all, and so the fruits of which they are the sole, specific price shall be lost to us irrevocably. And as hinted already, the fruits here alluded to are of a special character, and have therefore attached to them an emphatic singularity, a peculiarly significant type of value, which separates them very widely from anything we find elsewhere. There is here not only no substitute possible, but no approximation to such substitute. The contribution woman makes to society, the force she furnishes at this point as one of the elements of civilization, is simply and absolutely incalculable. It does not, indeed, build ships, nor construct railroads, nor sink mines, nor erect factories. It is not a bank, it is not an insurance company, it is not a corporation. It dabbles not in stocks, it declares no dividends. Up to this day, at least, it is not the national Congress; it is not even a state legislature. And finally, it lacks even the external dignity of organization, the peacockism of periodical display at formally summoned conventions, the noisy demonstration of a caucus, the stage effect of scenic dazzle and outside glitter. It makes its appeal to none of these; needs help from none of them : for it is an element of authority, not of force, its authority even resting not upon any human enactment, but demonstrated to us by its fruits, rather than by any outward symbols, any self-arrogated claims, any claims supported by the penalties of a broken statute.

And the law which I am now attempting to apply to the subject, bestowing upon us as it does this specific blessing through and by specific channel only, will here as rigorously as elsewhere insist upon the conditions. The source from whence we derive equivalents like these must be preserved punctiliously, and sacredly maintained in all its integrity, if we would hold on to the gift. We have it in our power to relinquish, if we will, the property we now have in this element of strength, this ornament of beauty. We may straightway scatter to the winds all the lessons of the past, become again like foolish children to whom the light of experience has not happened, and under the love of innovation and change, the temptation of novelty, or what not other motive, by a departure from the former arrangement, invite woman to new fields, new duties, new occupations. We may say to her, — for such would be the language of this contemplated reform, — "Up to the present time you have failed to contribute your part to the growth and prosperity of the commonwealth to which you belong. Cease to be the drones, the half-workers, you have hitherto been. Come down into this mire of politics, put your shoulders to the wheel, help along the triumphal car of progress. Inform yourselves on the current political topics of the day, enjoin it upon your "lords and masters" to bring home with them at evening the newspaper devoted to partisan strife, surprise him at the breakfast-table with the extent of your acquirements, demonstrate to him that Mr. A. and not Mr. B. is the man for the occasion. Brushing out of your way the toys of the nursery and the implements of household duties, go proudly and loftily forth to the evening caucus — now being yourself enlightened, and in turn enlightening others from the sacred rostrum; and when the day arrives on which you are to exercise the inalienable right, stuff your reticule with ballots and a smelling-bottle, off with you to the polls, elbow your way through the steaming ranks, and deposit your vote."

This, and much more like this, is the language addressed to woman by this wonderful reform. It is not enough that men should be besmirched by contact with the "beast," that their conscience should suffer foul injury as they mingle in the unhallowed strife. It is not enough that the slime of politics should leave its trail along other less consecrated paths, but it must creep into the sanctuary of our houses, infect with its pestilent odor the fragrance of domestic life, and divide the house against itself; for if the woman is always to agree with the husband, argue as he argues, and vote as he votes, what kind of a liberty is that now lately bestowed upon her! "*Procul, O pro-*

cul, este profani." Avaunt, avaunt, ye unclean spirits! Away, away from these abodes of peace and purity! Defile not these sacred altars with your polluted and polluting offerings. Afford not another illustration, more pregnant, more eloquent than any that has preceded it, of the folly of ignoring and defying this law of equivalents, more pregnant and more eloquent here than elsewhere, because here, more than anywhere, it has special application, here more than elsewhere its violation must be attended with special loss.

It will be perceived, without calling attention to it, that an exhaustive treatment of the question in hand is not being here and now attempted. My object has been only to bring it into the light which the view I am illustrating is calculated to shed upon it, leaving other points of equal weight untouched, because here out of place. As to woman's capacity for politics, and the value of any contribution she might bring to the State, supposing her conversion to such a purpose once complete, — this is a question that needs not discussion here. I might safely admit it, if it be insisted upon, without damage to the argument. But if the point were to find place here, then, before inquiring what might be the value of any contribution woman is likely to bring to politics, we must first know what the thing itself is worth which is to receive the contribution. And I think the answer must be, it is worth very little. That it makes great noise in the world, is a conspicuous thing to attract the gaze of the world, and that the world seems to move very much by its aid, is all true enough. But for all that, in the long catalogue of valuable equivalents, I incline to the belief that it is outranked by not a few, and that, being of comparative insignificance itself, it is incapable of receiving from any quarter a great contribution.

It will also be perceived that I have thus far examined the question chiefly in its relation to the State; its connection with woman herself, her rights, her interests, her duties, having received little or no attention. But an examination of the subject in its bearing upon the last-named point would lead to the same conclusion as that already reached. It would be found here as elsewhere, that whenever Nature provides a separate, distinct organism, whether spiritual or material, or both united, she indicates a separate, distinct economy as applicable to it, both as to its management and its capacity for good to others, and its own thrift and prosperity; and that by a strict adherence to, and following out of, such economy, we convert it into the highest service it is ever capable of. The great law, the great effort of Nature everywhere, is to preserve and multiply kind. It is so, because when kind is destroyed, the Equivalents of which it is the source are also destroyed. And if Nature did not make such effort, and arrange her laws to that end, it would be a confession that the original creation was unnecessary. We see this clearly, and readily acknowledge it, in the world of matter, and wherever we find a vegetable or an animal multiplying itself most rapidly and prosperously, there we decide is its true habitat, — its proper sphere. If under certain temptation we remove it from such, its legitimate soil and climate, if we attempt to convert it over to new habits, new uses, new duties, we understand perfectly well that we do it with some risk, with the certainty of some loss.

But kind in the spiritual world falls under the same law, and intermeddling here will be followed by results equally disastrous. Each and every mental endowment, each and every instinct, each and every emotional element, is a distinct kind, not less than is every species of vegetable, or animal, or mineral. It is ordained, not less than they, to meet certain great necessities, the place it is to occupy, the product of which it is capable, and its entire adaptedness for the ends it proposes, being ascertained and provided for under the general economy, with the same precision and certainty which we so readily perceive and recognize in the material world.

The great differences, then, which distinguish the sexes are to be surveyed in the light of this proposition. They rise to the dignity and importance of kind, even while depending chiefly upon degree. But to be preserved and made subservient to the purpose for which they were created, the laws that pertain to them must be observed.

I have thus far attempted only a general survey of the question, making use of such arguments as are supposed to be applicable to every state and condition of society. It remains to inquire whether these arguments derive any additional force from the peculiar type of civilization which prevails at the present time, and upon these American shores.

And I cannot better indicate the train of thought I desire to suggest as applicable in this connection, than by referring to the two types of civilization which are most diverse one from the other, — monasticism and industrialism. How these occupy opposite poles; how under the law of Antithetical Equivalents there is possible no equatorial blending of the two, but each must retain its own individual characteristics, and that too upon terms of surrendering something which belongs to the other; and how advantage would flow to the State by a certain interfusion of both, if such were possible, has been remarked upon already.

And which of these two types is now happening to us is plain enough. It has passed into a truism long ago, that modern civilization devotes its attention and its energies almost exclusively to material interests. Be the explanation what it may, the fact is plain that every new propelling power, come from whence it may, but serves to give increased momentum in that direction. It is undeniable that every new discovery, every successive invention, is at once subsidized into the service of the body, and made to minister to bodily comfort. There never has been a period in the history of the world when there was so much to invite the accumulation of wealth, or when such a passion could be so easily gratified. Nor is it a cynical or sentimental spirit which ascribes to these pursuits certain mental tendencies and habits of thought which need a corrective. Without claiming that they are in any sense degrading, it is evident that they make their appeal chiefly to the intellect. There is little in the ordinary paths of trade, and commerce, and speculation, to address the tender, emotional part of human nature. There is a battle, and hard fighting, but it is more sordid than chivalrous, — more calculated to harden the heart than to soften it. Nor is there here and now any reason for protesting against such a condition of things. But accepting it as it exists around us to-day, we may find in the fact a corresponding necessity for the antagonistic force which shall neutralize, or at least mitigate, some of the tendencies it brings in its train.

There is probably no one truth the world more fully accepts as matter of mere speculative belief than this, — that out of that part of man's nature which we term emotional springs a very large proportion of all that tells upon man's life. And yet the practical recognition of this truth can hardly be said to come fully up to the purely intellectual perception of it. On the contrary, there is very much to hinder such recognition. And more than this, there is very much in a hasty, superficial survey of society as it unfolds itself before our eyes, very much in its external exhibition of itself, which gives color to the idea that men generally associate depth and strength of feeling with weakness and an unbecoming unmanliness. It may be true, I doubt not it is true, that such a verdict is intended only to be applied to an outward display of such emotion. But in the very act of insisting that such display is indecorous, — at the same moment the decree is uttered which forbids all public exhibition of susceptibility, follows the inevitable inference, even if it be false, that some stain attaches to the thing itself. To feel strongly or deeply carries with it, in some sort, suspicion of infirmity; and as the great work the world proposes to itself to-day as its task chiefly concerns figures, statistics, calculations of trade and commerce, and as it is quite evident all these can go on their way without help from the emotions, nay, much better without their help, the result is certain enough, and evident enough, — strength lies in the head and in the hands, but weakness, not strength, lies in the heart. And it is quite evident that the error, which has thus got itself established in spite of pure intellectual convictions to the contrary, is not to be cured by arguments addressed to the intellect.

To recur, then, to the thought above alluded to, I remark that, differing as they do in very many particulars, the monastic is distinguished from the industrial type of civilization by special emphasis in these two points: the first named gives depth and earnestness to the emotions, and fosters a reverential spirit; and its estimates are founded more upon the development of man himself, and less upon his external achievements. It inquires what the man is, — not always and only what he does; what his own individual life is, — not what is the summed-up availability of the machinery that life represents.

And in view of these premises, instead of adopting the more usual form, and so pronouncing the great blemish belonging to American civilization to be its entire engrossment with material pursuits, I adopt this more convenient if not more logical form of indictment, and would say that the great necessity to American civilization is more reverence, as opposed to intense egoism and contempt of authority; and a protection from some quarter against the hardening, dwarfing, cramping influence of a too exclusive and too ardent devotion to a single pursuit. It needs something to interpose against its mechanical, automatic tendency, and so render it less matter-of-fact and more imaginative, less calculating and more emotional; in a word, to make it, not one-sided, but many-sided.

And the nearest approximation we make towards supplying this want is to be found in woman, both as furnishing the emotional, imaginative element, as helping in a variety of ways to keep alive a spirit of reverence, and as exhibiting and commending to our regard the great truth, that while action is not to be sneered at, it is not all, but that it is something to be a good man or a good woman. I have already in a separate chapter spoken of Reverence as an element which cannot be eliminated from the problem of American civilization without great loss. In an important sense it lies at the foundation of every organized society. It must find food, — must have provision made for it somewhere. Wherever we find certain accidents existing unfavorable to its development, whether in the political system, in an unwonted career of success, or what not, so that its voice becomes hushed and feeble, there exists the greater necessity of bringing into our service whatever tends to encourage it and promote its growth. Rightly regarded, such a gift would be among the greatest the American people could possibly receive. The positive blessings it brings with it, and those of a negative character it bestows by saving us from its opposite — Contempt, are beyond computation. It deserves to be called the great American want this day and this hour.

Now almost the only secular source for this gift remaining to us in anything like its original purity is woman. Most seasonably she offers herself to meet this exigency and supply this want. Up to this hour at least — what may be in store for us in the dim future I know not — she remains an object of willing homage. Alone of all the manifold elements of civilization which surround us to-day, she retains unimpaired her power to excite and to command our reverence. There passes no single hour of his life when man, and the society of which he forms a part, is not resting under this influence. If it be an inferior form of reverence when brought into comparison with that which flows from a recognition of Deity, it is the same principle; and as she is herself an object of it, so she is in a multitude of instances the means of directing man's vision and man's heart to the great fountain source, not of reverence only, but of other kindred sentiments.

And it need hardly be added, how woman, too, remains almost the only object to mitigate the idol-worship of money with which man prostrates himself to-day with more than Eastern devotion, and how she almost alone interposes between him and the golden Mammon which threatens to take him captive. Never was a higher truth uttered, a truth more intimately connected with the well-being of the race, than that which declares that civilization may be measured by the respect in which she is held. It furnishes a touch-stone nearly or quite infallible. As chivalrous sentiment is better than sordid calculation; as self-sacrifice is better than self-adulation, and devotion to others than care only for ourselves; as tenderness is better than cruelty, and gracefulness than rudeness; as modesty and purity surpass shamelessness and uncleanness; as love is better than hatred, and forgiveness than revenge; as reverence is better than contempt, and a religious faith is better than unbelief; nay, if it were necessary to say so, as even that upon which superstition feeds, and that which superstition bestows, is better than a cheerless, selfish, abandoned no-faith, — as all this is true, so is it true that we must retain at what not cost a high appreciation of woman herself, and of woman's gifts to us; and hence it follows, as surely as day the night, that woman must not only be enshrined in our holiest affections, but so far as possible must be held uncontaminated by the grosser pursuits which are necessary for men, and especially that, as to her special idiosyncrasies, she must be neither despoiled nor tarnished by contact with the pollution of politics.

The thought here introduced — viz., the special adaptedness of woman to confer upon one type of civilization — the industrial, certain marks and certain capabilities which are the natural result only of an opposite type — the monastic, and which, except for this accidental contribution, would be lost to us — might be still further extended. She in a variety of aspects typifies both, not only by virtue of natural gifts, and more diversified instincts, but also by being brought into less intimate connection with civilization as to its distinctive and peculiar development, and so more removed than men from its cramping, paralyzing, distorting influences.

Believing that the principles involved in this question are of paramount importance, I must ask the indulgence of the reader for a few words in conclusion. The present age is emphatically an age of drifting. Former anchorage grounds are abandoned; old landmarks are sinking out of sight. It seems not an audacious prediction, that the movement of civilization for the next half century will owe very much of its character — more than to any other single cause — to woman, and to her contributions as such, and mainly for reasons already alluded to. With so much that is purely intellectual, mechanico-intellectual; so much that is critical; so much that is automatic and arbitrary, — sentiment, imagination, docility, impressibility, cannot but fare badly, are faring badly already. But without these, what is a state, what is society, what would life be? Has it ever occurred to these innovators to estimate what would be the value of material wealth, however abundant, to inquire what money, be the quantity ever so large, would be worth, I will not say virtue and principle being eliminated, cast out of doors as so much surplusage, nay, as an embarrassment in getting money, but only that being lost to us which passes under the name of ornament, accomplishment, grace, tastefulness? Virtue, moral principle, a Christian life, are indeed worth a great deal more than these. But because they are worth more, it does not follow that these which rank second are good for nothing. They constitute almost the only hold we have upon very many. There are very many who might not think it a great sacrifice to lose religious faith, and the sanctions of religion, who would yet, should they once bring themselves to contemplate such a result, shrink from surrendering all that society owes to mere outside decorum, to external accomplishments, and to the courtesies and amenities of life. Many men value order, commercial integrity, domestic purity, and wholeness, — in short, all the virtues that pay, that contribute to a well-ordered state, and to the peace and prosperity of society, — who care little for principle for its own sake, little for religion in itself considered. But these lesser graces and these inferior gifts are threatened, quite as much as religion itself, by an all-engrossing pursuit of wealth, and it well beseems us to put the question suggested above, if we have not already done so, what is it to us that our storehouses are filled with costly merchandise; what is it to us if we become, as we promise to become, the richest people the world ever saw, — if, having obtained the means to gratify our emotions, we have no emotions left to be gratified? Are we ready to accept deliberately and in words what our lives seem to declare, and so become machines and nothing else, — to grind in an everlasting prison-house, only to produce results we may never taste of? Because it is a bad thing to be poor, and a good thing to be rich, are we to forget why this is so? If it be so, if to have more money than our neighbors is what we are content with, let us know it and be done with it. But let no man complain, having made his choice, that he is disappointed.

Of one thing we may be certain, — that a higher truth, a truth more closely connected with man's interests, was never uttered, than that which declares man is a religious being. It certainly does not mean that he must be a sectary, or adopt certain formulas of belief; but it has reference to certain wants in his nature which the emotions only can supply. In the early stages of society, in the days of fable and of superstition, however these may conduct to error and to stumbling, these wants are readily provided for. In older and more advanced civilizations these disappear, and then it is that the religious instincts of woman help to supply man's necessities. Differing from him as she does in so many particulars, she differs more than all in this: she lives nearer heaven. To her, heaven is a realization in a sense far, very far, beyond what happens to him. Her imagination and her sensibilities combine to localize heaven.

Its gates of pearl, its walls of jasper, its streets of gold, are to her a reality, not so much from intellectual conviction as because the idea harmonizes with, and makes provision for, her emotional nature. There she thinks of a long line of pious ancestry being gathered. There she expects to be reunited those tender ties that are ruptured on earth, — there to join the angelic host in anthems of praise to her great Deliverer. And by her magnetic influence she draws others into the same circle. She becomes an interpreter, or at least a conveyer of divine truth, to those about her.

And where her influence falls short of this, she still feeds the emotions. If she does not make man religious in the strict sense of the term, she is a forming influence in his character, which in the very nature of it admits of no substitute. And on the whole it seems matter of deep regret, that it should ever have come to have place in men's minds, that in the absence of restraints furnished by religion, there is positively no foundation for character to rest upon. Teach a man that without religious principles he can have *no* principles, and he will soon learn to strive for none. And at a period when cavilling, sharp-eyed criticism abounds, which, if it beget not scepticism, makes men gravitate towards indifferentism; at a period when material interests so almost entirely absorb men's attention, — it would seem especially unfortunate if restraints of an inferior order should be denied their proper place and value. Even vice itself is not always and only reproved, but gets sometimes refreshed, and plunges into its filthy delights with new ardor when it has lately returned from looking at virtue. The coarse man never so enjoys his coarseness as when he has just had his fling at purity. The man whose soul has been eaten out of him by greed of gain never more chuckles over his smartness, and so makes his vice pander to his enjoyment, than when he has just turned empty away from his door the needy applicant for relief. So inexorable is the law of duality; and if virtue goes her way with quicker step and renewed delight as she contemplates the wretchedness of vice, so vice owes something of its zest to its being brought into contrast with virtue, and would, oftener than it now does, tire of itself if it were always compelled to look only at its own features. Is it a hard saying, that virtue is thus made contributory to vice? So there are many hard sayings for man, and must be always, seeing that for him the law is limitation and not absoluteness. And herein the necessarian theory, rightly understood, has its advantages: it represses romantic hopes, instructs us that there are no covenanted blessings unmixed with evil, and teaches us, even in our lowest estate, not to take to ourselves utter condemnation, since limitation is itself weakness, and weakness, however in other respects painful, is not sin.

But this is falling into digression. What I am saying is, that there is very much which by common consent has a value for man not resting upon any sanctions of virtue or religion, but only commended to our regard as being useful, or ornamental, or pleasurable, which at the same time we must be prepared to surrender, unless some provision be made for the imaginative, and graceful, and æsthetic element. That is to say, even on the supposition that religion is a fable, and virtue only an idea, we are still admonished that the pursuit of money only — the consecration of our energies to the sole object of amassing material substance, nay, that mere intellectual activity, would in the end inflict upon us severe loss. And it is here, I think, that will be found a very cogent argument in favor of widening, rather than of erasing, the line of demarcation which separates the sexes. Even on the supposition that society and woman herself would receive a benefit by admitting her to participate in politics, it would be out of all proportion to the loss that would thus ensue.

The language so constantly upon the lips of "Woman's Rights" advocates reveals as belonging to them a fundamental misconception of the whole question that is utterly fatal to their reasoning. "To elevate woman,"— this is their stereotyped formula. And what they mean by this is, not to make her a more perfect woman; not to take a specific gift which Nature has given us, and, by fostering and cultivating it in its own direction, develop it into its legitimate and therefore most valuable uses; it is not to coöperate with Nature and, accepting her laws, to avail ourselves of her assistance,— it is nothing like this they intend when they talk about "elevating" woman; but it is to act against Nature by bringing her into a nearer resemblance to man. Having thus far, it seems, failed to reach her true level, she is to reach it hereafter by copying after and imitating the great lord and master of creation.

Thus the first stepping-stone in their argument is an open, direct insult to the object of their professed philanthropy. They at least are dissatisfied with woman as she is, and charge her with not having fulfilled her destiny, not having discharged her duties, not having contributed an honest share towards the commonwealth, as man has done, and therefore — such is the precious *sequitur* — she must be made more like man, who, it seems, has no such delinquencies to answer for!! As well, nay, far better, might woman "get up" a movement for elevating man, and if, attempting this, she should follow the notable example given her by these her champions, she must bring man into a closer resemblance to woman; the result of the two movements being simply this, to bring about an interchange between two absolutely opposite forces, and to convert them from their natural to an unnatural use. A similar attempt in the physical world, by which an unnatural conversion should be attempted, would not be a whit more absurd, nor attended with more mischievous consequences.

Such attempts have been sometimes made, and by wind-blowed bladders tied to their feet men have tried to walk upon water. The laws which govern in the material world are too well understood, and too generally accepted, to encourage largely such experiments, or to furnish believers in them; and it is only because men do not equally recognize the operation of law in the moral universe that sciolists and empirics draw such crowds to witness their less manifestly convicted follies.

And it is upon the loose holding of this latter class of laws, even by those who stand aloof from this movement, that the advocates of it found their hopes of success. Not a few of its opponents, if called upon to explain their opposition, would go off into a somewhat general harangue about household duties, and woman's fitness to attend to them; others would speak of her æsthetically, — of her gracefulness, her taste, her fine social qualities; and still others, making a somewhat nearer approach to the truth, would speak of her as furnishing the emotional and poetic, as opposed to the intellectual and more prosaic, elements in society. Nor, indeed, are these by any means to be omitted from the summing-up. They are not to be lightly dispensed with, the loss of them, even if this were all, far exceeding anything we are likely to receive in exchange. But what I desire to say here is, that this is not all. There remains this, — that woman is an interpreter to man of vast stores of knowledge, or, to speak more accurately, of wisdom, which but for her would forever remain undisclosed. And this gift of hers is not so much a sharpening of his vision as it is the purifying of it; or, still more properly, it is the bestowing upon him of a new vision, and introducing him to thoughts, and views, and experiences to which his own less impassioned, less sensitive nature would never conduct him. Nor is this a result of accident, and so capable of being disregarded without loss. It is ordained to be so; and even were there any reason to wish it were otherwise, that can never be. There is no substitute for woman's instinct. It is the *open sesame;* not, truly, for everything, but for very much that man now gets access to, — the one sole key to many a lock whose intricate wards would forever defy all man's cunning, all his efforts. And as instinct is better than the highest reason, that is, in its appropriate fields, in that it never misleads its followers, which the highest reason often does; and also for this, that it discloses very much that reason could never discover, and is moreover little affected by accidents of the external, — so woman, excelling man in instinct, is made superior to man by this her gift, just as really, and just as certainly, and just as importantly, as man is her superior by virtue of any gifts that typically belong to him; while this superiority, depending upon a natural provision, is something whose loss cannot be atoned for by a substitute.

By the law of her nature, then, woman is an intellectual force in society, first by virtue of her higher emotional organization, thus imparting vigor and enthusiasm, and so success, to very much that would languish under tamer and more sluggish efforts, and indeed keeping alive what would else perish outright; and then also by her gift of instinct, by which she becomes to man, in the full sense of the word, an interpreter. And while, viewed in the light which the Law of Equivalents sheds upon the subject, the truth here insisted upon appears to greatest advantage, since by that law we are reminded upon what exceedingly nice points success frequently turns, and are reminded, too, how, failing to put into requisition the sources which Nature supplies, we fail altogether, — still, aside from this particular view, and not depending upon it, woman is here revealed to us as an agent of such value, nay, such indispensable necessity, that all intermeddling by rash experimenters deserves our sternest reprobation, and should be met with our most earnest opposition. For when it is said that woman is an interpreter to man of much he would not otherwise attain to, the idea is included that, to retain this office, she must remain steadfast to her womanliness. Instead of being "elevated" by an imitation of and a closer resemblance to man, she is, then, most elevated when the distinctive marks and qualities which separate her from man are brought out most prominently, and preserved most punctiliously; just as any and every organism is wrought out into its highest honor and value when it is by appropriate culture retained for its own specific and natural use. And that sufficient hardihood should ever have been found to deny so palpable a truism would excite nothing but wonder, only that we have often before been made to see how nothing is sacred against enthusiastic innovators, and no absurdity is too great to be swallowed by those who become unduly enamored of a pet project.

Astronomers tell us there are stars so distant that their light has not yet reached us. If the same is true of the moral universe, if truths in moral science yet remain for our discovery, such result may be expected through woman's instinct, and her openness to delicate impressions, which her more sensitive organization eminently fits her for receiving.

If, then, woman remains steadfast; if, by giving her sanction thereto, she continue to recognize herself as the standard and as the sustainer of a high moral sentiment, as the sole source of certain chivalrous emotions which neutralize opposite tendencies; if she will but continue to exercise the authority which at present belongs to her on the side of right living and right doing,— she will accomplish far more both for herself and for the state than she can ever do by joining the army of voters. But to do these things she must remain a woman, and then her cast-off slipper shall have in it more influence for good than a whole regiment of woman imitators can ever exercise at the polls. If she but remain steadfast; if she will be content with rewards attested by no outward, public blazonry, but only by the approval of her own heart and her own instincts; if she will listen to herself as her own true monitor, and turn a deaf ear to these modern oracles whose only merit is that they offer something new; if she will be guided by that clear-seeing eye of hers, and then let it rest lovingly, and affectionately, and with a true guardian's faithfulness, upon the great interests committed to her care,— all will be well.

I have thus brought the question of Woman Suffrage into the light of a particular law — the Law of Equivalents. And little remains to be here added. It may be objected that I have taken a mere utilitarian view of the subject, and have confined the inquiry to the single point of woman's usefulness to society, leaving her own rights and interests uncared for. I humbly submit that this is not so. I have, indeed, endeavored to make it appear what are her distinguishing qualities, her prime excellencies, and to show upon what terms the state must receive at her hands what she has to bestow, if it receive them at all. But it follows none the less certainly, that she at the same time consults and provides for her own happiness by occupying the place which these qualities eminently and identically fit her for occupying. Her own interests, not less than those of the community, forbid a conversion to illegitimate uses. I now pass on to consider the institution of the Family in connection with and under the operation of this law.

CHAPTER XVIII.

THE FAMILY INSTITUTION.

FAMILY — the very word itself is redolent with sweetness. It is a holy, yea, a wholly divine word. It fairly outtops every other word in the language. It is not so much an apothegm as a treatise, not so much a treatise as a text, not so much a text as a sermon, not so much a sermon as a poem; carrying us back, by the very mention of it, into scenes fragrant with blessed memories; the name of the Saviour himself, if I may say so, borrowing a new lustre when brought into this connection. The heathen poets, and their successors in modern times, understood well its value. The parting of Hector and Andromache, "The Cotter's Saturday Night," the passage in "Paradise Lost" beginning "Then came still evening on," "Enoch Arden," and a host of others, attest the truth of what I am saying.

And the word has all this significance, not by mere accident of association, but because it typifies the noblest and the holiest emotions which remain to man, — emotions whose tendency is to draw him away from the defilements and the dross of earth, and lift him into the skies; to the pure gold and the stainless glory of heaven. If we ever catch a glimpse of the "Beautiful City" through its open gates, it is when we follow with earnest vision the objects of our love, who, taken away from the family circle, have been admitted to a membership in the great family above. The silver clasp, the golden hyphen, which connects earth with heaven, is found precisely here; here, if it happens to us ever, we not only hope, but believe, that the soul is immortal; here, if ever, we pass through a consecration that fits us for communion and fellowship with those who, having preceded us, are waiting to welcome us to the abodes of the blessed.

And these things are so established by a wise ordination and a firm covenant. The grace that adorns, the love that consecrates, the confidence that illuminates, the sympathy that endears and compacts and fortifies, the common interest that consolidates the little community around the family fireside, are no result of human contrivance, but have their roots deep in the heart by a divine preappointment, and, as cannot be doubted, for a specific end. And hence it happens that we have here placed in our hands equivalents, offering which we are sure to be the recipients of commensurate rewards; for what comes to us by virtue of law can never disappoint us. If, then, the law seems rigorous in its exactions, we may find consolation in reflecting that it is faithful to its promises. The recompense is beyond a peradventure, no man having ever yet paid an equivalent in this kind on a mere venture.

Nor will the significance of this law we are considering be anywhere more strikingly exhibited than in the Family institution; for, while a neglect of it nowhere else entails a greater loss, so, as matter of fact, it is nowhere else more constantly ignored, more wantonly despised and flagrantly set at naught. It outranks immeasurably all and every other instrumentality, because it really lies at the foundation of them all. It is no disparagement of the Church, with all its concomitants of Sunday schools, benevolent societies, and other like machinery, to say of it that, as compared with family influence, properly directed and utilized, it occupies only the second place.

And this importance grows out of the fact that we have here furnished one of those great equivalents for which no substitute can be invented, no compensation can be devised. It is a price to be paid by us in kind, and to be paid at a time certain; its absence no more to be atoned for in the coming years by any extravagant outlay whatever; the deferred payment no more possible to be made up for at a future day, than that the river, which has flowed away and been lost in the sea, should be recalled by the miller to grind his corn. If the iron in the hands of the smith becomes too hard to receive the desired impression, it may be again thrust into the glowing forge, for time enters not into the equivalent here; but, as has been noticed elsewhere, time is an equivalent in very much that concerns our highest interests.

And what this family influence, regarded in the light of equivalents, is, or should be, will be best seen by bringing it into comparison with other great forming, moulding agencies. In the world at large, everywhere outside of the paternal roof, even in the much-boasted school-room, everything is matter of *contract;* and almost the only inquiry raised has reference to mere externals. Society demands action, because drones are unprofitable. Society demands pay, because by that it lives. It bestows its caresses and its smiles, to say nothing of more substantial favors, upon those who minister to its comfort and its pleasures by their acts, — by their achievements, great or small. Laborers all, — the illustrious and the ignoble, the man of genius and the patient drudge, he who works with his hands and he who depends upon his brain, — all are sure of their reward. And so it will be always. But society at large pays no man for what he is, takes no account of him for what he is. It is what he does, what he performs, what fruit he bears. And the same is true of the State in its capacity as guardian and as administrator of the laws. It has to do with overt acts, while the Church itself, so far at least as its disciplinary action is concerned, is shut up to the same rule.

With all this the Family is in striking contrast. It is not Society, it is not the State, it is not the School-room, it is not the Church. It differs from them all. It has in its hands gifts which all of them united cannot bestow. I propose in a few words to bring it more particularly into contrast with each of these, and to show, first, —

Wherein the Family Differs from Society.

As noticed already, man finds himself the subject of various wants. While many of these have attached to them a mere money value, there are a vast many others which money will not even assist in procuring, each of them having its own distinct source of supply, and to be had from such source only. And as the payment is various, not homogeneous, so also must be the sources from which it is to be drawn. In proportion as we first fully understand what these sources are, and are made to perceive their applicability, their appropriate action, and their specific value, and then proceed to exhaust their capabilities, just in that proportion we evidently make our nearest possible approach to perfection; just in that proportion we get what escape is possible for us, from the evils that afflict and the burdens that oppress humanity. This is evidently the length of our tether. There may be spacious fields beyond, compared with whose spreading extent, and whose fresh, tempting luxuriance, our own trodden circle seems all barren, all narrow, all desolate; but they are not for our occupancy, our exploration, our enjoyment.

As just remarked, there are certain great sources which may be called by distinction primary, each furnishing a separate Equivalent. And to first understand, and so in the end fully exhaust, these sources, they must be brought under analysis; and to perceive the specific value of either one of them, we must compare it with all the others. How, then, does the family differ from society at large? In very many particulars, a few only of which I propose to bring into notice here. And first of all I observe that Society, while it tends to one-sidedness itself, that is, to a set in a certain direction, opposes individuality of character. If the expression is allowable, it averages the members who compose it, who, rolled like a pebble on the beach in its everlasting swash, incline ever to sphericity, not angularity of development. Coming along constantly with its stereotyped maxims, some of them true, many of them false; with its whole cumbrous machinery, — traditional lore of etiquette, arbitrary conventionalisms, its long train of artificial enactments and restraints, its blandishments and its cajoleries, its love of flattery and impatience of rebuke, — coming along with all these and much else like these, it represses with mandatory frown whatever seems likely to jostle its settled routine, or in any way to interfere with its prerogatives, now firmly established by long prescription. Its own self-complacency, its love of ease, its compliant temper, its egoism and self-laudation, are at once disturbed and rebuked when brought into the presence of rugged honesty, of truthfulness, heartiness, and sincerity of temper. These are the sharp points which tear and lacerate its dainty, carefully preserved cuticle,—which ruffle into unseemly disorder the soft, glossy feathers it has taken so much pains to arrange.

So far the result is positive. There is another principle which negatively or passively tends in the same direction,—the imitative principle. Thus society no sooner invites the symmetrical, spherical development in its members, than themselves, on the other hand, readily respond under the influence of imitation. Singularity, however an occasional instance of it may be met with, either real or affected, for the great mass is intolerable. By no means confined to matters of dress, the tyranny of fashion prescribes with almost equal rigor what we shall think, what we shall say, how we shall talk or smile or walk; in fine, determines the very manner of our whole life. We must imitate, not originate. We must follow, not lead. We must see what others do about us, and how they do it, and then do the same thing in the same way. This is society; this is what society offers in the way of Equivalents, and to be sure it is nothing very brilliant. I am speaking here, it will be understood, of moral Equivalents; for when it comes to those which are the price of material gifts, society is full-handed enough.

But introducing now the other picture, that of the family, the contrast is so plain that he who runs may read. I do not mean that there are no points of resemblance, — that the family sanctuary, secure within its closed doors, bolts out every jarring sound, every sight that offends, and so entirely escapes the infection. It is enough for the purpose of the present argument, if the difference now claimed to exist be found at all. And it may, too, be as conveniently observed here as anywhere, that I have in mind what lies within the province and the capabilities of the family institution; not by any means asserting that it always, or even for the most part, comes up to the mark.

Under any well-arranged family government, then, one of the first duties is, instead of quenching particular aspirations and repressing certain aptitudes and particular tastes, to encourage and cultivate them. I incline to believe that in American families this is done to a very limited extent. I say in American families, because, as it is the fashion for every man to know everything, and as he is ashamed to say "I don't know" to any question put to him, no matter how far removed the subject from his own study and profession, the attempt is to meet this exigency. Any specific culture, any effort directed towards a development in a specific direction, is supposed to be unfriendly to this demand for encyclopedical knowledge, for a Jack-at-all-trades capacity. We might get a useful lesson from our English cousins in this particular. With them, the fashion is to make searching inquisition into idiosyncrasies and special aptitudes, and so to promote that individuality of character which it is the tendency of society to destroy; nor does an Englishman seem to regard it as matter for reproach should it appear there were some things he had not yet learned.

But this inquiry demands personal attention, and is attended with inconvenience. It is thus shifted over to others. Teachers, books, and other apparatus that so cheap a thing as money will procure, are at hand in abundance; but the father's duties at the office or counting-house are of paramount obligation, at least he thinks so; and the "searching inquisition" into peculiarities of mind and heart, so that what is in excess may be restrained, and what is weak may be strengthened, and what is a special aptitude may be encouraged, fails to be made. The Equivalent is there, ready at hand, certain, as law is certain, to receive in due time its reward, if it only be appropriated. But if not thus converted to its proper use, then by no juggle, by no turn of luck, by no gift of a friend, by no answer to fervent prayer even, shall the reward be reached. The father made his choice; he has what he paid for, what money could buy. If this child of his has suffered loss because by inattention certain natural gifts were not developed as they might have been into a high order of excellence; if this other child has failed of the encouraging word from time to time to expel that distrust of its own powers which so haunt it and beleaguer it about; if that other has missed the timely admonition against headstrong passions and hurtful vices, — let not him complain that there were some things his money did not secure.

Now, in making provision for and accommodating itself to these diversities, these differences in tastes, in emotional types and tendencies, the family, where all these are freely displayed, finds itself differing very widely from society. Even the weaker members, furnishing sometimes occasion for sympathy, become elements of strength; and while free play is allowed for the emotions, and the sensibilities are deeply stirred, truths and sentiments find a lodgment in the heart which remain there forever.

But were there nothing else to distinguish the Family Institution from Society as a source of Equivalents, the three great sacraments of marriage, birth, and death which belong to it would in themselves suffice. Each of these places in our hands Equivalents whose value we have no means or power of estimating while they still remain in our possession; whose value, indeed, we rarely think of estimating, so closely and so constantly do they dwell by our sides. But as each of them gives birth to emotions that could reach us by no other channel, so each of them makes us acquainted with new truths of which we could otherwise have no experience; for a new emotion can never happen to us from any source, much less from sources like these, without bestowing upon us a new truth, or, which is the same thing, imparting a new value to old truths. Subtract from society the variegated contributions it receives from these three great family sacraments; let the marriage bells no more ring out their merry, joyous peals, and so the new ties that are formed and the old ones that are severed no longer be known; let infancy, whose helplessness affords an object for our care and food for our sympathies, whose trustfulness and whose innocence rebuke our suspicions and our frailties, and whose satisfied joy in the present reproves our exacting and grasping temper; let infancy and the light it brings into our households be extinguished; and, more than all, let Death be spoiled of its sting, shorn of half its terror, and thus discrowned as king, since, by there being no family circle for it to invade, it has lost both its territory and its empire over our hearts; let these chastening, spiritualizing influences cease; let the poetry of Death be withdrawn, and its solemn music no more fall upon our ears, — let these things be so, and society would then indeed become the sham, the empty mock, it is so often declared to be: nor would it be an extravagance of speech to say, that a city through whose streets the slow-moving procession, with its solemn hearse and nodding funereal plumes, never passes, would be nearly or quite ready itself to be buried out of sight. So that, here as elsewhere, out of Death springs Life; and if the Family Institution had no other gift for us but this one alone, that it bestows upon Death such a significance and clothes it with such a power, its claims upon our regard would be past calculating.

CHAPTER XIX.

WHEREIN THE FAMILY DIFFERS FROM THE STATE.

THE somewhat extended remarks already made under the head of Political or Governmental Equivalents, render it unnecessary to devote much space here to contrast the State with the Family Institution, as a distinct forming influence in civilization. There are evidently very many points of difference, or, to speak more accurately, there is very little they hold in common; but the great, distinguishing feature is, that while the State by no means denies the value of authority, it is still compelled, in its administrative capacity, to call to its aid force, in a degree quite beyond what is true of the Family. A very large proportion of its effective sanctions partake of this element; there being, perhaps, no better criterion by which to estimate the degree of perfection to which a state has politically attained, than that which inquires how far it is able to dispense with force, and to depend upon the element of authority only. But in all well-regulated families, force is second and authority first. And the difference here indicated is closely connected with another: the state takes note only of overt acts; motives, all the inward hidden springs of action, being quite beyond its cognizance, except, indeed, so far as the classification and definition of certain crimes is concerned, when the motive may be inquired into. So, again, the state administers justice, and settles conflicting claims of its subjects; indeed, directs all its movements in the gross and by a wholesale process, any discrimination or letting-up in favor of exceptional cases being for the most part impossible. A severity, if not injustice, is thus made at times to characterize its proceedings, which the more elastic and considerate temper and structure of the family never exhibits.

Then, to maintain its own honor, and to preserve its own integrity, has precedence over all other duties resting upon a state. Depending as it does for its prosperity upon the welfare of its subjects, their interests are after all second only in importance. Indeed, the modern doctrine is now well established, not only that the State should be separated from the Church, but that the fewer the points of contact, and the less intimate the connection between the state and its subjects, the better it is for both; and the less consciously the individual is made to realize that there is a state, the more perfect may it be pronounced. Nor is our attachment to it at all like that we bestow elsewhere. Pride is a sufficient reason for desiring its growth and its honor, while a sense of its importance in protecting us from injury, is the chief foundation of our regard for it. If patriotism were always unprofitable, exposing the subject of it frequently to loss, but never bestowing advantage upon him, we should hear very little of it; and even at the best, it deserves a place only among the inferior and doubtful virtues.

This summary at once indicates the general nature of the Equivalents of which the State is the source. They manifestly enough belong to a very different category from those furnished by the Family; and I now pass on to inquire —

CHAPTER XX.

WHEREIN THE FAMILY DIFFERS FROM THE SCHOOL-ROOM.

IN the competitive rivalry of the various institutions of learning which offer themselves for our patronage, no claim is oftener put forward than this, — that the discipline and general management is based upon, and includes the advantages of, the family arrangement. How far this claim ever approximates even a fulfilment, I need not stop to inquire; allusion being made to it here because it furnishes a concession to the truth of what I am seeking to enforce, — that there is a natural and therefore essential difference between the educational gifts which the school and the family are severally capable of bestowing. Be the approximation greater or less, it is admitted to be the result of special effort directed to that end; it is conceded that the family has naturally its own capabilities and its own adaptedness for yielding a certain discipline and a certain development, which, so far as they may be appropriated at all by the school or the academy, are to be appropriated only upon terms of borrowing. This is evidently the concession. This evidently means that the family is the source of certain Equivalents which the school-room does not naturally furnish, and therefore furnishes them, if at all, in a diluted and imperfect degree.

And when it is considered how very often it happens that parents imagine full provision has been made for the education of their children, and so their own responsibility is at an end when reasonable care has been given to the selection of schools and school-teachers,— when we are made not unfrequently to see this point comfortably disposed of and settled from month to month, and from year to year, upon the same principle that the paid-for services of the butcher and the baker leave nothing unprovided for in their departments, it will not, perhaps, be regarded as labor lost, when the attempt is made to survey the question in the particular light our subject seems calculated to shed upon it.

And in the first place it may be remarked, that these two institutions occupy absolutely different fields. It is not merely that, both directing their efforts to the same end, one accomplishes that end better than the other; but each has its own distinct province. The very machinery and implements of the school-room declare at once its province. To impart knowledge, to convey instruction, and, professedly at least, to exercise and discipline the intellectual powers, — this is its business. And it does this after its own fashion. It has its set formulas. It provokes emulation. It stimulates industry, and encourages the formation of strict habits of thought. It proceeds by arbitrary rules. And it is sheer matter of contract, — so much Algebra, so much Greek, for so much money. It administers education by the cart-load, and "finishes" it, as a builder finishes a house. It rarely suffers to escape from its recollection the periodical visiting committee, nor the day of examination. It announces its edicts, utters its precepts, goes through indeed the whole established routine, with a certain mechanical order and regularity; bestows its degrees, graduates many excellent scholars, and is in its place an exceedingly useful and altogether indispensable agent.

But for all this, it is not a family. It might be very much more than it is, and still it would not be a family. Skilled as it might become in the art of "borrowing" just alluded to, it would be at last only a borrower, and very much would remain quite beyond its reach even in that capacity. And one principal ground of the distinction is this: the results witnessed and obtained in the schoolroom are chiefly those of manufacture; those in the family are results of growth. The pupil, under the eye and directing skill of the teacher, is made into an accomplished scholar, and increases doubtless his intellectual stature: but we still say of him, and with perfect propriety, he has been built up into what he is; the child, under the eye and supervision of his parents, grows into a living man.

And the two processes have very little in common, and any loss that results from a defect in one of them can never be atoned for by a more thorough prosecution of the other. They fall within the category of Equivalents, each yielding its own fruit, and the father having quite as much right to expect his son to become a proficient in Greek because he has received lessons from a dancing-master, as that the school-room should furnish what only the family influences and training can supply. For the distinction between growth and manufacture is quite as broad, and quite as important to be observed, in the spiritual as it is in the material world. The distinction, I readily admit, is not straightway enforced by evident and instant penalties in one case as it is in the other, because failure and disappointment do not so instantly follow, and are not so signally and indisputably the result of, a violation of law in spiritual matters, as in things which only concern our material interests. Indeed, it is because the connection between cause and effect is not so distinctly revealed to our eyes in the class first named as it is in the other class, that we are in reference to them surrounded by doubt and perplexity, and, with all the careful forethought we can exercise, are still betrayed into fatal mistakes. And it is at this point identically that the subject we are considering gets most of its significance. For if the laws applicable to these two departments were alike understood, and were esteemed to be equally certain in their operation, we should never need to be reminded that, although a school-room may furnish very excellent scholars, it cannot make men; for manhood is something that grows, and can by no possibility be had by a process of manufacture.

The conclusion to which we are conducted is, that education is a twofold result — first, of growth; second, of manufacture, — that it is the province of the Family to supply the first, and that the School or the Academy, however complete in their own sphere, are not a substitute for it. What are the peculiar and essential conditions of such growth, we may not tarry here to examine. It must suffice to say that they include personal devotion, personal watchfulness, personal minuteness of attention, personal sympathy; none of which a public system of instruction is at all competent to furnish: and they furthermore imply the presentation and enforcement of motives which the family, in virtue of its peculiar authority and its distinctive position in the great aggregate of educational forces, is eminently fitted to yield. It is an Equivalent which may not be dispensed with without the inevitable loss.

And here, doubtless, we are to look for the explanation of a not uncommon disappointment, as unexpected as it often seems inexplicable to the subject of it. Nothing is more common than to meet with men who set a just estimate upon stipendiary services in their business engagements, and who accordingly select certain duties for their own personal attention, but who in other matters trust to the very gold they have so lately despised, — a mere "stipendiary" teacher of youth, for aught that he can see, being quite good enough for that purpose, and withal very convenient. And he therefore pays the gold. Measured by the rules of the counting-house, gold is a good payment, and he pays it, bountifully, ungrudgingly. By that rule, as we have already seen, gold cancels all demands, so that there be enough of it, and even a lack of it may be atoned for by some other commodity. But gold, however capable itself of excusing its absence by a substituted recompense, was never yet received in lieu of personal service and personal sacrifice, where these are made a part of the price; and the father who thinks that stipendiary services are good enough in the education of his children, which he has already rejected as untrustworthy in his business, need not complain in the end if he receives only that for which he paid the price. He cannot escape the law of Equivalents.

CHAPTER XXI.

WHEREIN THE FAMILY DIFFERS FROM THE CHURCH.

I HAVE thus in the preceding chapters pointed out certain characteristic marks belonging to the Family, when brought into comparison with Society, with the State, and with the School-room; and have attempted to show how it furnishes Equivalents which belong to neither of the others.

It will probably be equally apparent upon slight reflection that, while there are many more points of contact, and while a closer bond of sympathy subsists between it and the Church, than have been disclosed as belonging to it when contrasted with the three forces above mentioned, it still occupies a field of its own. That there is a mutual interdependence of these two institutions one upon the other, that a highly prosperous and flourishing condition of one of them can hardly be looked for while the other is depressed, will be readily assented to. The foundation of both rests, if not upon altogether identical, certainly upon analogous principles. They both make their appeal to a similar class of motives. They both address and stimulate similar emotions. They both inculcate the cultivation of the moral sentiment; both insist upon personal responsibility, and both thrive as they best succeed in implanting and enforcing the maxims and the rules which contemplate these ends. Nor would the Church have been so often described under the similitude of a family unless there had been very many and close points of resemblance.

And that the agreement should be so close, still leaving each to fulfil certain duties to which the other is unequal, only again illustrates the law under consideration. The Church itself not only concedes all that is here claimed, but by recognizing and enforcing it — by insisting, as it constantly does, upon the specific Equivalents furnished by the family institution — it makes known one of its own strongest claims to our support. It understands very well that the family is, in an important sense, the foundation upon which itself rests; that it is the instrument by whose aid it accomplishes very much of its own work. And if this perception of the value of this institution, thus turned to account by the Church, could only be imparted to certain sciolists in social science, and to reformers everywhere, who promise order and beauty but give us only chaos; if political philosophers and venturesome experimenters, who think to discover the panacea for human ailments in some one or another of their own ingenious contrivances, would only take hint from the Church, and so accept this truth and act upon it, in the sense that she accepts and acts upon it to-day, — a blessed jubilee would dawn upon the world quite beyond our present power of conception. For while to-day the Church exhibits a marked singularity in thus recognizing the family as not only an efficient but an indispensable ally in its particular field of operation, the State would no less find its account in appropriating to its use the same instrument. Does the Church direct its aim towards the cultivation of a spirit of reverence as underlying the system it would propagate, and does it find its own efforts in this direction greatly assisted by the encouragement this spirit receives in the family, the State is no less dependent upon the same element for its prosperity and perpetuity, since subordination thus becomes a result of authority instead of force. And so of other qualities which might be named that ripen under the same propitious influences: they are of value to the State and to society in the same degree, if not for precisely the same reason, that they are of value to the Church.

But it is time to proceed with the inquiry, wherein these two institutions differ, so that we may understand what we owe specifically to each. We have seen already that they are dependent one upon the other, — that they both subsist upon principles nearly identical.

And one very striking point of difference suggests itself at once: the Church attaches excessive importance to belief. Unbelief comes to be reckoned as one of the most deadly sins. There is no way in which it can wholly avoid this. Creeds, dogmas, are its staple, not so much from any special voluntary choosing of its own, as from a necessity that belongs to the case in the nature of it. It gets here the conditions of membership. Here it finds the distinguishing badges that mark its various sects. No small portion of its care is directed to the preserving of the boundaries which separate these various divisions and sub-divisions one from the other; the incentives to zeal and activity flowing from this source being very considerable.

And, indeed, in some periods of its history this matter of belief has been almost the only thing considered; an extreme liberality having been extended to the minor points of deportment, so that an external profession of faith was made in accordance with the prescribed formulas. Nor can this excessive sensitiveness in this regard afford any cause for surprise. In those periods when intense bigotry and a tyrannical spirit of proselytism were the almost sole incentives to religious zeal, and when the prevailing type of theology attached a much greater importance to a mere speculative belief than has been characteristic of later times, the external profession met every demand, and as a matter of course the conduct and behavior of the believers came to be reckoned of small consequence. And when these baser and impure motives were subsequently exchanged for others of a less odious and objectionable character, and in theory at least belief came to owe its value to the fruits which it was supposed capable of yielding, — a correct life being insisted upon both as an evidence of sincerity and for its intrinsic value, — there still remained much to exalt this element into a very prominent place. Unbelief has always been the one great enemy to be overthrown. From this quarter the Church has always encountered the most formidable opposition; and that it should regard the battle as nearly won upon the defeat of this its arch-enemy, is not unnatural; nor is it any more unnatural that it should embrace its opposite with peculiar ardor of affection.

Now admitting, as I have done, that there is in the nature of the case no alternative to the Church from this exacting temper on the score of belief, and not intending it as an imputation derogatory to its character or efficiency in its own field, it is still evident that an institution like the family, for instance, which is under no such necessity, has for many purposes a great advantage over an institution which is thus encumbered. Equivalents of great value, as we have already seen, turn upon much nicer points. And the psychological analysis which the question invites would seem to be one of very considerable interest. A moral development conducted under a system which meets the subject of it at the very threshold with sharp inquiries upon matters of doctrinal belief, and that, too, upon confessedly mysterious subjects, and which inquisitively anatomizes mental experiences in relation to the same mysteries; which critically weighs and balances certain emotional frames — which follows up the earlier impressions with incisive attack and jealous watchfulness, — must plainly enough differ in very many and important particulars from a development which goes on under the more accommodating, and amiable, and elastic arrangement as it exists in the family, — an arrangement so far removed from what is mechanical or the result of contrivance, that it may be spoken of as self-adjusting, rather than as adjusted by anything external to itself. The remarks made in a previous chapter find application again here: the whole process is one of growth. Belief itself, instead of being introduced into the mind from without by certain apparatus of argument and of logic, and so to an extent a product of force, springs up, then, spontaneously in the very centre of the soul itself. It is not so much a result of effort directed to that specific end, but is something included in that more general and invisible process by which certain mental operations and experiences conduct the subject of them unconsciously, but certainly, to the appropriate issue.

Thus not only belief, but every other mental or moral product, — the entire development, is not a something bestowed upon the character and added to it, but is incorporated and intertwined with it; innumerable fibres growing up into one harmonious, homogeneous whole. And it is this principle of spontaneousness, assisted and guided by wholesome precepts, and saved from excess by patterns all around it inviting imitation, which more than all else besides gives to the family institution its precedence over all other educational agencies.

CHAPTER XXII.

CONCLUSION OF FAMILY INSTITUTION.

I CANNOT prevail upon myself to dismiss this part of my subject without once more asserting its intimate connection with the prosperity, if not indeed ultimately with the very life, of the nation. If any one thing more than another would shock my faith in a possible improvement to man's condition and destiny as a gift of this our American civilization, it would be a fear lest the variegated restraints and wholesome influences which now flow to society, from that respect which the family institution has hitherto inspired, were about to be lost.

There is much to-day lying upon the surface, and frequently meeting the eye, which seems to indicate, if not an increasing laxity of sentiment as to its sacredness, at least an inadequate estimate of the value of the family institution, considered both in its relation to individual manners or as a governmental element. I have not now in mind that disposition already remarked upon, which finds aliment for the state exclusively in organic law, constitutional formularies, and all the generally recognized machinery of government; but I allude to a certain truancy to principle, winked at if not fashionable in these days, which is derogatory to the intrinsic claims of the institution itself. Toleration of perfect freedom of opinion, and a full expression of the same, is part and parcel of the American system, nevermore to be surrendered. But toleration, especially as regards certain subjects, is encouragement, and latitude of sentiment is no sooner allowed than it is invited. Schism, not fusion, is the great temptation which liberty and intellectual activity inevitably offer. Under such a condition of affairs, new sects and new parties multiply only as a natural sequence; and as they spring up spontaneously, the result of little labor or sacrifice, and subject their followers to no martyrdom, they often collapse and pass into forgetfulness as suddenly as they appear.

The free-love speculations, however, which have been advanced of late years, seem unfortunately endowed with greater vitality, or at least to be finding favor, and ripening into organized forms, which promise a greater permanence; closely connected with which, if not thus originating, is the movement in favor of "Woman Suffrage." I do not mean that all the advocates of the movement last named coincide with the "Free-Lovers;" but the tendency of their tenets is in the same direction, and perhaps even is the more dangerous of the two, since it is far more insidious in its approach. One is as hostile as the other to our real interests, and both, it is to be hoped, will in the end be indignantly repudiated by the American people. I am not ignorant how in certain quarters what is now being said will provoke only sneers; and it is not impossible that an importance is here claimed for the subject which will appear unduly magnified even by those who have no sympathy with the new order of things I am now deprecating.

But " eternal vigilance is the price of liberty;" so runs the maxim we all profess to receive. Undoubtedly, — eternal vigilance. But where is this vigilance to be expended? In seeing to it that certain political texts are not tampered with; that certain carefully worded guaranties are religiously preserved; that the children in our schools be early indoctrinated with patriotic sentiments, and, by a frequent comparing of our own form of government with any other the world has yet seen, be taught to believe that a " form of government " is something altogether apart from the people who live under it; that it makes them, and not they it; that, except for the inconvenience of the thing, it might as well be located in Japan, or Terra del Fuego, and indeed better, if so be any saving of expense could be thus reached, — is that what is meant by " eternal vigilance "? If so, we seem to be tolerably safe, for such price is easily paid. There is nothing in all this which money will not do, which money has not always been doing. But the price offered seems hardly commensurate with the magnitude of the expected return. It lacks the true nature of an Equivalent; whatever can be procured with, or very greatly assisted by, money only, except in commercial matters, being by that very circumstance of a suspected genuineness. It is not the open, avowed foe we are to hold at bay by visible ramparts of constitutional enactments and such like, but it is the sapper and the miner, who, under some Free-love badge or other, gets admission into the citadel, — that is to say, into the hearts of the people; for there is the citadel, which once surrendered, the rest may go as booty to camp-followers or what not.

I have said above that much appears upon the surface to suggest fears of a growing disesteem of the family arrangement. I believe that up to the present it is to a considerable extent a "surface" demonstration. I believe there are thousands and tens of thousands of happy families scattered all over these illimitable acres, who, if they are not making the most out of the relation which it is capable of yielding, are yet, in theory at least, holding fast to it as the great anchor of their lives; and who are in fact, if not always consciously, thus appropriating to their use and enjoyment the highest instrument Heaven has bestowed upon them, both for their individual content and prosperity, and for the welfare of the state. A Roman minister in Julian's cabinet, pleading for the preservation of the temples threatened with destruction by that emperor, used the following striking and beautiful language. "The temple," he said, was to them (the peasants whose cause he was pleading) "the very eye of Nature, the symbol and manifestation of a present Deity, the solace of all their troubles, the holiest of all their joys. If it was overthrown, their dearest associations would be annihilated. The tie that linked them to the dead would be severed. The poetry of life, the consolation of labor, the source of faith, would be destroyed."

I believe there are thousands living to-day of whom the same language might be used in reference to the family, — thousands who find here the mystic bond that holds them fast to the principles and sentiments of virtue; here a motive and a reward for honest toil; here an incentive to honorable exertion; here a "temple" of worship which strengthens and purifies the soul, and elevates it into a contemplation of, and an alliance with, something better and higher than the perishable objects of sense. And that there is any considerable number who are willing to pattern their lives, socially and morally, after European fashions, which politically they so agree in condemning, I will not believe, until compelled by more and stronger proof than is before us to-day.

CHAPTER XXIII.

EDUCATION — ARSENALS OF LEARNING.

EDUCATION is greatly insisted upon to-day by the American people. Reckoned as it is among the chief factors in any civilization deserving the name, it is supposed to be more than ever of paramount importance under that particular type which they themselves represent. The attention it has received, the discussion it has begotten, the learning it has from time to time enlisted in its service, are beyond computation. Is it thought for a moment by anybody that the estimate of its value thus indicated is extravagant? Great as has been the labor expended upon it, vast as have been the contributions it has received, and searching as has been the thought devoted to its support, is there found a desire in any quarter that there should be an abatement in these particulars? Or, on the contrary, is there not abundant evidence that the demand is rather for increased devotion to this subject; even questionable methods, or at least methods which fail of a unanimous approval, such as the Blair bill in Congress, sometimes finding advocates, so strong does the current set in this direction?

Is it supposed by the writer of these pages that by introducing education into the family of Equivalents, and so bestowing a new name or title upon it, any additional, intrinsic value is to be got for it? So far is this from being true, that, if he did not hope that the inquiry now set on foot would tend to illustrate his main purpose, he would have hesitated to introduce it at all; and that hesitation would have been still further increased by the fact that incidental mention of the subject has been made already in the preceding chapters. A separate notice of it here, however, may not be entirely without justification.

And if education may claim to be called an Equivalent at all, the first question which naturally arises is this: What is it an Equivalent for; or, in other words, what are the contributions it makes to civilization, how does it make them, and in order to render the full tale of which it is capable, what must it include? Very much that it is counted upon to do, counted upon, too, with a confidence that is never disappointed, it is easy to enumerate. It strengthens and develops the intellect. It equips men with certain weapons indispensable on the arena where their mental powers are to be brought into play and fully tested. It enlarges their power of thought. It widens their intellectual horizon. It cultivates and enriches the imagination. And it tends, at least in some respects, to quicken the emotions, by furnishing them with a food they would otherwise never taste. Men thus become fitted to make returns to society which we gladly and gratefully receive, feeling, and really being, all the richer for them. So the instruments and the various machinery education makes use of for this purpose — the school, the college, the university — come to be styled, as they properly may be, arsenals of learning.

And I suppose that when we speak of education, this is what habitually we have in mind, viz., its purely technical or academic sense. The formula above stated covers for the most part all that we expect from it. And if it bestowed upon us nothing more than this, it might well deserve to be called an Equivalent. If we depended upon it for nothing beyond this, it still might well claim to be one of the foundation stones in our American system. But is this all? Does it stand us in stead for nothing more than this? This thing called education having been thought worthy to be reckoned an Equivalent, is this the extent of what it has to bestow upon us? To the careless observer there is a great deal to fix one in that idea. Very much that addresses the sense helps in this direction. From the humble schoolhouse up to the proud university, the eye is made ever to rest upon her habitations, where Education is, figuratively at least, supposed to have her special home with all her utensils about her. Here is her laboratory, here her operating table, her crucibles, her retorts, and the rest of it, by whose aid the process goes on. All these become the external emblems, the visible symbols, the veritable badges, of the order; while periodical exhibitions, great gala days, that take place while the process is in progress, and the granting of ribboned diplomas at the end of it when the happy subject of it all has "finished his education," make, as it were, the parade dress which bestows a certain éclat upon the performance from which such great results are expected. Bigness, and all that represents bigness, and not by any means what bigness represents, — how that captures us, even the best of us, as the phrase goes, who ought to know better! Strange enough, this bowing down before such a clay image (clay not only as to its feet, but up to the very crown of its head), rendering it homage! The chemist would tell us that a single drop of water, as such, means more than Niagara, as such, with all its thunders.

Is this a light way of treating the subject, with a view to deny, even by insinuation, the just claims of education, even when surveyed under the aspect here presented, — claims so long and so universally accepted as genuine? Not at all. It is said here only by way of getting a hearing for this question: Is this the whole of it? Having bestowed so much upon us, are its entire capabilities as an Equivalent exhausted? Does its office and all that it is adapted, and I might add intended, to bestow upon us, end here? I submit that it does not end here. I submit that when we make special selection of education as one of the main pillars in our political fabric, to fully justify that choice, and so fill out its claim to be an Equivalent, — for I must remind the reader once more that this is my present aim, — we must include something more than is set down in the above schedule.

And this brings me to the point of asking, what is education? In a single word, it is to develop the man; the whole man, and not a part of him. To a considerable extent, the conditions of such development are provided for as already explained, and "arsenals of learning" dot the land. For a certain portion of our coast-line defences they make ample provision, and so to this extent they are Equivalents. How, for purposes of the argument just now in hand, it is not necessary to insist that education does not fill up the measure of its gifts merely in imparting knowledge, in storing the mind with facts, goes without saying. It is hardly worth while to stop here to attack that error, an error nearly or quite exploded already. My meaning here is quite apart from that, goes altogether beyond that. It asserts this,— that the process and the fruits of education are not confined within certain walls thereto dedicated; but unconsciously, and yet not less certainly, the process goes on and the fruits are plucked outside of these sacred walls;

goes on spontaneously, without the intervention of stipendiary agents, of any cunningly devised apparatus, or of any particular thought of ours thereto directed. Is it objected that what falls into our hands thus unconsciously, no special effort put forth on our part, must be of small value? If so, let it be replied that the objection only shows that the full meaning of the law of Equivalents has not been reached. Rigorous even to seeming cruelty as is this law, insisting as it does that the coin be not debased but genuine, it is no niggard. It does not dole out its gifts with a parsimonious carefulness. Giving does not impoverish it. Ever at our side, nothing escapes its vigilant eye. From no forgetfulness, from no fatigue of an overworked hand or tired brain, from no exhaustion of vital force of any sort, does it ever withdraw or intermit its activity. As has been remarked already in another chapter when not speaking of education, very much we could ill afford to dispense with falls into our lap without conscious effort on our part. Habits carelessly adopted; the force of example supplemented by the principle of imitation; experience, sad and disappointing or otherwise, chiefly perhaps the first named — all this, and much else of the same sort, are what this hard schoolmaster takes sharp note of, making always inevitable and discriminating return therefor. Historical illustrations to this effect might here be cited beyond number were this the place for it.

To return, therefore, to the point I am after. A certain large and very important part of what in the gross constitutes education, and especially the education which would at all justify our so building upon it as a governmental factor, — which would at all justify us when we so fondly speak of it as the keystone in the political arch, — I say a very large part of all this we get by a process of gradual, spontaneous accretion. In a single word, it is a process of growth and not of manufacture, and any estimate which omits this from its summing-up is a wholly incomplete estimate, and by so much we fail to reduce into possession what awaits us if we pay the price. By so much we underrate the value of education as an Equivalent.

Am I in all this seeking only to magnify my subject, dressing it up in borrowed feathers which do not belong to it? Is any claim here set up to a new discovery even? Should the complaint stop short of this, it may appear to many to be at best a mere question of definition, and when all is said and done, it may be held to be only the threshing of old straw which yields no grain, — complaint grave enough, it is true, when it is considered how much of that kind of work is being done already. But — to find a figure of speech in my subject — since a new text-book is held in high repute, whose claim often consists chiefly if not wholly in its novelty, perhaps a new *flail* may be allowed to share in that somewhat equivocal merit.

And unless what has been thus far herein attempted has failed of its purpose altogether, it has sufficed to remind us that education is complex and not simple. It is of a twofold nature, deriving its value from a twofold source, and surrendering up for our use the entirety of its gifts only when both sources are applied to and drawn from. The two sources are so distinct in their nature that they may be said to have absolutely nothing in common. They have their origin so wide apart, what they yield up and bring to our doors flows through such different channels, and they are so unlike in their several properties and in the administration of the same, that the absence of one hardly suggests the absence of the other; the presence of one does not imply the presence of the other. Hence evidently, to cast upon one that for which the other is the true Equivalent, is to rob ourselves of an inheritance which nature has provided.

Another branch of the subject falling under our notice in this connection comes into view when, no longer treating of education as itself an Equivalent, and so a benignant distributer of precious gifts, we come to inquire how this agent may become ours. It is relied upon to pay us bountifully. What must we pay for it? It stands us in stead as an Equivalent not to be dispensed with. What is the Equivalent we must be prepared to offer in order to make it ours?

Plainly enough, questions like these, to examine

which only an entire treatise would suffice, can receive here only the most general notice, and find only a partial answer, for which the most that can be hoped is that it may be suggestive. Education being itself, as we have just seen, of a twofold nature, so clearly must the price to be paid for it be twofold. For that part of it which for convenience sake has been styled academic, " arsenals of learning" being its true symbols, it would be superfluous to enumerate all that is counted upon. It is catalogued already in everybody's memory. It may, however, be remarked that here, as so often occurs elsewhere, the Equivalent includes variety of payment. The apparatus now in ordinary use, all the equipments long recognized as essential, such as suitable text-books, " improved," if so runs the prescription; libraries; comfortable, well ventilated, well drained buildings; competent teachers, and much else of the same sort, must be at hand. With all this in abundance, is nothing still wanting? Have we thus paid the whole Equivalent? Only remarking that by " competent teachers " something more is intended than anything a mere perfunctory service, however faithful, has it in its power to bestow, — a point not to be dilated upon here, since it is allotted to us to put up with perfunctory service more or less everywhere, — the question just put may receive affirmative answer as to that part of the process now being considered. As to the other part, its helpful but too often forgotten if not despised ally, which for convenience sake may be called extra-mural, it is evident at once that the field of inquiry, which such more comprehensive view invites us to explore, is too vast, includes too many intricate problems, and involves too many mooted points, to be even entered upon in the discussion now in hand. A single thought, however, may be worth a moment's attention.

Embracing, as education does under the aspect of it here exhibited, the whole life of man from the cradle to the grave, and so demonstrated to be an Equivalent which comprehends within itself everything that acts upon that life; moulding it, feeding it, directing it, unfolding it, building it up, sanctifying it or degrading it, rendering it a beneficent patron or a destroying angel, and so made pregnant with bright hopes or dismal forebodings as to the future of the republic — responsible for all this, the question becomes more than ever interesting as to what is to be its own future. Having in mind the half century just expired, — an epoch far outrivalling any that has preceded it in its stupendous march, — what have we in hand to help answer this question which we lacked in the opening of it? Has the wonderful advance in scientific inquiry, whose deft, searching finger has lifted the shroud from so much that till now has been sepulchred in death, brought any new light here? Has education as a science received new impulse, new contributions of any sort, in the same sense as is true, for instance, of chemistry and astronomy?

And passing by for the present any particular, more specific accessions it may have received from the source here indicated, may it not be said, without exciting uneasy fears in any quarter, that by the aid of this searching finger, heredity, taken note of in a more general sense, has been made to fill a much larger place in men's thoughts than it did formerly? Liberated from the leash of manifold thongs which once held it in check, disembarrassed of a prejudice which had its foundation in much that is now obsolete, it has come to the front to make its voice heard, for good or for evil, in all the councils where humanity is henceforth to get a hearing. Does it admit of any practical application whatever to education, so that it, too, may be reckoned an Equivalent? Under its guidance, for instance, is there any reason to hope that distinctive traits, special aptitudes, mental or moral idiosyncrasies; too much or too feeble nervous development, resulting in a hurtful precocity, or in its opposite, dulness — any reason to hope that these and other similar points will be more carefully studied and provided for? Or are we only to be again reminded of the insurmountable barrier which separates the organic from the inorganic, and while we rejoice over the rich fruits we gather from discoveries in the kingdom last named, must we be left to mourn as aforetime over the meagre results yielded by the first named?

It is doubtless too early to seek a definitive answer to questions like these. But from the exhibition of education here attempted in its twofold aspect,— the academic and that which has been designated as the extra-mural, — the inevitable corollary seems to flow, that man's external surroundings and his individual inherited germ, if not the main or only factors, constitute at least very important ones in determining what the whole final outcome shall be. These, multiplied one into the other, will make return, to fully comprehend which will repay abundantly any investigation we may bestow upon it. It is hardly necessary to say that there is no thought here of offering anything even by implication that shall touch the question of free-will or necessity. Unfortunate, however, would it seem to be, if, by reason of the opposite views entertained on the subject, and the hot strifes thereby engendered, we should be deprived of any possible legitimate lessons to be extracted therefrom.

What, then, is the conclusion, if any, we are led to by the foregoing presentation? Simply this: Education, as an Equivalent, as already insisted, includes in its full, proper sense everything that man comes in contact with; everything that addresses him in his whole complex nature. Excepting only that which the subject of it took at his birth, it is responsible for his outcome, be that what it may. The two factors, and the only two, unless we include the supernatural, are the original germ and the educational influences it is subsequently subjected to. The experiment having been conducted up to the point when these two have been multiplied one into the other, the whole inevitable result is reached, incapable of addition or subtraction.

Into what prominence, then, does not this Equivalent become exalted? If, however, in our summing-up of the gifts it has it in its power to bestow, we have in mind only that part of it which is here denominated academic, we greatly overestimate its claim to belong to the family of Equivalents at all; while on the other hand, if we think of it in the more comprehensive sense above explained, it will be found holding an office whose paramount importance the wit of no man can magnify or reach up to. Instead of the first-named furnishing a substitute for this broader use and application, it is more true to say that, in proportion as it (the academic) is conducted on a more liberal scale and is more widely diffused and bestowed, in the same proportion has the extra-mural, its supplement, a heavier responsibility cast upon it, and so rises in the scale of Equivalents, because, while more is demanded of it, it will still be found equal to that demand, unless hindered by our own apathy and neglect. In other words, the moment a new leaven of intelligence is infused into the masses, bestowing upon them an increased momentum, there arises the necessity for an increased guiding power to accompany such change.

Under one motive and another we are provoked to cast a horoscope of the destiny which awaits a civilization supposed to be in advance of any that have preceded it; to learn what is in store for a people who to-day are prosperous and happy; to know the fate of a great nation almost fabulously rich in its own resources, and spreading out its arms to gather tribute from outlying regions. Nor does it require a divining-rod — a prophet or the son of a prophet — to predict that, when the day of its fall from these lofty heights shall be fixed, the determination of that day will be found to have been retarded or hastened according as the twofold Equivalent herein described shall appear to have been more or less appreciated and made use of.

CHAPTER XXIV.

RESULTS.

It will be perceived from the foregoing exposition that the subject treated of is capable of almost indefinite expansion. It follows man wherever he goes; it stands by his side, whatever may be the path that his energies may select for their exercise. It covers a very wide and diversified field, — a field which includes everything that stirs the human emotions, everything that falls within the range of human industry.

It might have been expanded into much greater length. Embracing, as it does, so numerous and variegated a class of objects, it is hardly to be expected that any single mind will accept each individual thought or illustration. And even by those who find but little to condemn, and who do not recoil from receiving the general truth sought to be conveyed, it may be objected that the view is calculated to give a discouraging estimate of man's capacities; to depress, rather than animate to exertion; to produce stagnation, rather than stimulate to action.

But rightly considered, I submit that their influence is the opposite of all this. Faith and Doubt are the two great elements in the human constitution. As these severally preponderate or are quenched, activity or inaction must always prevail. And it is at once evident that whenever we make that certain which has hitherto been uncertain, or in proportion as we do this we strangle Doubt, we revive and establish Faith. The traveller who has lost his way in the wilderness is relieved by being set right, even though upon terms of a longer journey than he had been anticipating. So if it be demonstrated to us that there are certain fixed Equivalents to be paid for the enjoyment of a certain class of objects, even though such Equivalents may be difficult, nay, sometimes impossible of attainment, still, if we are thus assisted in the selecting, and so in the appropriating to our use, of these Equivalents, it would seem we suffer no loss from such demonstration, but contrariwise get to ourselves an advantage. Our hopes may, indeed, be somewhat chastened, and may never rise to so high a point. But what they lose here they more than recover by a steady, uniform flow, and this it is of which Faith is begotten. We may be taught to expect a more limited success in certain departments, and the field of operations may be more circumscribed; but an elasticity of movement is attained which never attends upon constantly alternating influences, when discomfiture and disappointment rob the heart to-day of the high hopes which yesterday's success inspired.

And if those noisy agitators who palm off their worthless wares upon society, if those seers who continually prophesy smooth things, are to be regarded as the true benefactors of the race, then there is no reason why the counterfeiter, and the coiner of base money, should not come in for similar praise. To the man who has a debt to pay, or a purchase to make, it is doubtless far from pleasant to find that his notes or his coin is spurious. But the lesson, at least, is not lost upon him. He soon becomes an "expert," and the whole tribe of counterfeiters give him a wide berth; and if we were equally interested in an opposite class of objects, where not money, but something very different is an Equivalent, we should find "experts" multiplying very fast in this field too, and with happiest results.

The following is not an extravagant summary of what the subject includes: —

I. It proposes a test which is applicable to every enterprise the heart of man can conceive. It divides between the practicable and the impracticable, and so suggests that wisdom which teaches us what to accept as the limit of our attainments. It directs our attention away from feverish dreams of what might be, from yearnings after unattainable gifts, from extravagant hopes and Quixotic schemes, and invites them to more sober views, more correct estimates, more fruit-bearing enterprises.

II. It invites a discriminating habit of thought and of estimates, and inasmuch as wisdom itself is seen to be divisible into different kinds, each severally adapted to procure specific return and no other, and seeing that even Wisdom must bring in her broad palm the identical price, it teaches us to expect that equally nice and strict conditions will be insisted upon elsewhere, as the only terms of success.

III. It brings home to our thoughts, and to our more perfect apprehension, the important truth, that there is nothing absolute for man; that he holds the full, perfect Equivalent for nothing whatever; that only the charlatan or the sciolist offers to-day, or predicts as possible in the future, a perfect and complete remedy for the ills and the distempers which afflict humanity.

IV. It hence teaches that there will be in the future, as in the past, much to endure; and that he who instils courage, and fortitude, and hardihood, is a more real benefactor of the race than he who endeavors to dispense with these elements by holding out encouragement that they will be no longer needed.

V. It teaches us that comparatively slender contributions should be accepted and gratefully received in the moral and social and political world; and also in all scientific departments that have to do with organic life, either animal or vegetable; since it is evident that the Equivalents for progress here, in the very nature of the case, are limited by more mysterious laws, and so are to a great degree unapproachable and inaccessible.

VI. It affords a lesson of humility found nowhere else. Pride, in all its varied forms, receives its death-blow at the hands of this law, for, measured by it, very much that pride builds upon becomes of small account. The gold of the rich man, except indeed to buy other gold; the learning of the learned man; the eloquence of the eloquent man; the argument of the strong man; the very wisdom of the wise man, — are of secondary value as direct Equivalents. They are hardly more than helps towards procuring Equivalents, doubtless of great value, and not to be depreciated, much less spared; but they do not occupy the first place. All united, they cannot bestow upon us those gifts of which Time, or Faith, or Conviction, or Earnestness, or Sincerity, or Reflection, or Honesty, or Self-respect, or Self-control, or Self-denial, or Self-culture are severally the conditions. All united, they cannot do that for a man he can do for himself, — nay, must do for himself: they cannot make him learned, or wise, or strong, or eloquent, or virtuous, or pure, or honorable; all united, they challenge our admiration chiefly, and not our homage and our respect, for these we award to the man himself, and not to his properties, be they what they may.

www.ingramcontent.com/pod-product-compliance
Lightning Source LLC
Chambersburg PA
CBHW030020240426
43672CB00007B/1022